ANTON COAKER

All the usual bullocks

A glimpse into the life of a peasant farmer

Foreword by Anthony Gibson OBE

First published 2011

© Anton Coaker 2011

Published by Anton Coaker
Edited by Sue Viccars
Designed by Simon Lloyd

wood@anton-coaker.co.uk, www.anton-coaker.co.uk

Acknowledgements

The material in this book has been gleaned from various organisations and publications for whom I write, including the National Farmers Union (both in their magazine *British Farmer and Grower* and in a blog on their website), the *Western Morning News*, and *Dartmoor Magazine*. Some has appeared in the various Newsletters and Journals of The Galloway Cattle Society, The Belted Galloway Cattle Society, and the Riggit Galloway Cattle Society, and some is drawn from private correspondence and emails.

Thanks go to all of these sources for kindly allowing the re-use of my material in this publication.

Some material is reprinted as it was first published, and some has been revised; some of it is out of order. The organisations listed above do not necessarily endorse or condone the content, views, or animal husbandry methods detailed in this book.

Thanks are also due to the many individuals who have helped and encouraged my efforts. Anthony Gibson is high on the list, always there with positive input and useful breaks. You're a gent, Gibbo.

And thanks to my lovely, lovely wife Alison, and the kids, without whom I would be in an even worse state.

Unless otherwise indicated, all photographs are by the author (including the front cover), or Alison Geen.

Disclaimer

British Library Cataloguing in Publication Data.
A catalogue record for this book is available from the British Library.

ISBN 978-0-9570953-0-4

Typesetting and origination by Edgemoor Publishing Limited.
Printed in Great Britain by Short Run Press Ltd, Exeter, Devon.

FOREWORD

Anton Coaker is that rare combination – a practical romantic. And by that, I do not for one moment mean sentimental. His writing – of which this book offers a delightful cross-section – could almost be used to define the description 'down to earth'. He confronts head-on, with no holds barred, in words as in life, the inevitable misfortunes to which a Dartmoor hill farmer with a saw mill and a direct meat sales business on the side will inevitably be heir: the bloody-minded Galloway cows (and, despite what he claims, there really is no other sort), the rank bales of silage, the broken-down lorry, the prolapsed ewe, the tree that falls the wrong way.

But his adventures must always be seen against the backdrop of a deep pride in what he is and where he comes from. Anton is a hill farmer to his muddy, diesel-stained fingernails. And a hill farmer, what is more, who has all of the qualities that you need to survive on a rough old patch of Dartmoor: an innate business sense, a feel for the land, limitless hard graft and, perhaps most of all, that almost indefinable quality called stockmanship. Anton has it in spades, and it shines through in his writing.

Then there is Dartmoor: 'my mistress', as he calls the moor. He loves Dartmoor, her people, her livestock, her traditions, her way of life, her 'cloak of peat upon her granite bones', with a rare passion. It was at the Dartmoor Commoners' Council that I first encountered Anton, and was struck immediately, not just by his practical knowledge of farming on the moor and his grasp of the law of common rights, but by his sheer respect for the place.

Anton is an acutely observant writer, with a keen intelligence, an often oblique way of looking at life and, especially when he is exposing the idiocies of agricultural and forestry red tape, a sharp wit. His run-ins with officialdom make for wonderful reading, and will strike a chord with every farmer and forester who opens this book.

The glossary is a gem. 'Dartmoor pony – walking precursor of salami' is a particular joy. What with that and Anton's inimitable writing style, if you haven't learnt yet to 'speak Dartmoor' you certainly will have by the time you finish this book. And maybe to 'think Dartmoor' just a little bit, as well.

Whether it is his farming, his forestry and saw mill, his travels, his beloved Riggit Galloways, his Dartmoor characters, the joys and trials of family life, the vagaries of farming politics or his encounters with bureaucracy, Anton Coaker writes about it with zest, colour, perception and humour. You will enjoy this book. I can absolutely guarantee it.

Anthony Gibson OBE
October 2011

INTRODUCTION

I've always enjoyed writing, having corresponded with various far-flung pals for many years.

Then, after writing about my very painful and public involvement in the 2001 foot and mouth debacle, I was kindly asked to write a bit more professionally.

The emotions were very raw for some time, and it showed (I deliberately haven't included any material from back then). Frankly, my family and I have mostly moved on, and hardly want to relive it all. I only mention it now to help set the scene for you. References to the flocks and herds I live and work with, and my evident issues with authority, might then make better sense. (One day, perhaps, I will write down how it went, and the fantastic back-story of the livestock I lost.)

As time went on I was asked for additional output for different publications and we increasingly realised that there was ample material for a compilation. And here it jolly well is. Much of it is borne of my observations of what goes on around me as I muddle through life. Some of it might make you laugh – some won't.

I apologise to non-farming readers for the inclusion of technical/vernacular farming references and terminology. There's a glossary at the end of the book which will help, but you may have to guess your way through some of it. Perhaps your enjoyment will be the greater for it.

My mistress

I have a mistress. My poor wife knows this well, and has always recognised that she'll reluctantly play second fiddle to my mistress, and will probably never come between us.

My own mistress is a difficult character. She makes demands of me that leave me exhausted and emotionally drained when I have to attend to her needs, but then occasionally sends my heart soaring like nothing else. She can sooth my soul when outside stuff is dragging me down, and the only thing to ease the tension is a long sojourn with her.

I have to jealously guard my place with her, as others covert our relationship, and everyone marvels at her attire. The cloth on her back sometimes stops you in your tracks, mouth agape. Her stark beauty and tempestuous moods have inspired artists of many genres.

Secretly, in my heart, I know that she has others, but that diminishes not the special relationship we share.

My mistress, if you haven't guessed, wears a cloak of peat upon her granite bones. Rain beats upon her brow, and seeps out of many springs, to run to the sea. She both succours me, and keeps me in my place. Such a rapport builds over years, although many more are called than she chooses. I am proud that I have so far managed to maintain my place at her side. (The analogy falls down a bit when I admit I inherited my interest.)

Should I be foolish enough to count the lambs I'm going to be selling from this year's crop before they are in the trailer, she chuckles. Then she rains and rains on them until their ears go all moth-eaten, and they want nothing more than to spend all eternity in her lap, becoming flecks of wool growing into the grass.

Just about any plans I make that involve her must absolutely defer to her haughty nature, or crumble before her response.

You may be in such a relationship yourself. If you are, you'll understand, and I hope your time together brings contentment. If you not, well, you'll probably never know.

Deep Swincombe *Sue Viccars*

WINTER 2007/2008

Dear George

I do hope this letter finds you in good health.

Thanks for the loan of that bull, 'Hercules'. He is, as you rightly said, a fine beast, whose obvious presence and impressive stature certainly do justice to his long and illustrious pedigree. Although I never got to see the facts and figures behind his ranking in the league tables, I'll take your word for it that his potential is right off the top shelf.

I do, however, take exception to the fact that I rather suspect you might have underplayed his 'feistiness' somewhat in your description.

As you know 'Drover Derek' organised the transportation of the bull. You must be aware of this, as I understand that it was a piece of your jacket that still adorned Hercules' left horn as he leapt clear of the wagon's ramp. (The hank of fluorescent lycra adorning his other horn remains a mystery. Derek does admit that some cyclists beside the road seemed very agitated, when viewed in the mirror, and that Hercules did have a horn sticking out of the ventilation gap at the time. Derek says he'll avoid that stretch of road for a week or two.)

What to do about the jet of green stuff that was expelled as the lorry passed the queue at the bus stop in Mitchell Hampton isn't clear. Derek thinks the bull must've coughed at the same time to have covered such a large group.

Oh, and Derek says not to worry about the smashed-up parting gate, he's got a spare, although I believe the owner of the heifers at the front of the truck is anxious to have a chat about something. (Indecently, Derek asked me let you know you'll need to find someone else to do your work. Apparently he and his family are emigrating any day now.)

On arrival, it would have been nice to have been able to get to know Hercules a little better in the yard. On advice though, we'd backed the lorry up the gate, straight into the meadow where the cows were awaiting his gentle affections. Unfortunately none of them seemed of interest, as Hercules didn't actually make it through the gate into that meadow. Instead he barged past Bob and I, and cleared the hedge opposite. This took him through Miss Pinkley's goats, which were quite startled, but otherwise unharmed. He cleared the hedge at the far end in one leap, not realising that there was a 10-foot drop into Church Lane on the lower side. He certainly seems to be made of sterling stuff, George, as he was straight up again, off down the lane heading towards the village. The post van that cushioned his fall wasn't up and about quite as quickly, but I'm sure they have insurance for that kind of eventuality.

Meeting the milk tanker in the narrows by The Grange slowed him up. (Bob had caught us up with the quad by now, and we all three had piled on.) When the driver tooted his loud air horns in a jocular fashion, as if to say 'Go back you silly bull', Hercules seemed to take offence and rammed the front of the tanker. That silenced the air horns, and I'd say he managed to hole the rad as well, because the Scania was bleeding green fluids when we moved off again.

Not liking road traffic much, the bull had smashed through the gate into Mrs Pomfrey-Hawker-Siddley's paddock behind The Grange. I do hope that wasn't the expensive Thoroughbred she got down from Newmarket. Seeing what Herc did to it as he went past I phoned the hunt kennels on my mobile. While I was on the phone Bob could hear the screams and splash which could only have come from 22cwt of beef passing briefly through the swimming pool Mr P-H-S installed last summer.

Knowing the post and rails aren't too good against The Vicarage we took a shortcut then, emerging just in time to see him surface from the vicar's garden, still wearing some of the patio furniture, and thumping down into the churchyard. The vicar wasn't at home to be worried about his garden, he was next door at work. He certainly seemed worried for the wedding party which Hercules briefly joined – Jack Harman's daughter, and the Clinkerbone lad, you'll recall. Nice young couple I thought, and she was hardly showing at all. There was a certain amount of hilarity as Herc tried to get in the family photos at the lych-gate (which, to be fair, already needed a bit of repair in any case). Well, they'll never forget their big day! Who'd a thought 'ivory' would go so well with splatters of green.

We lost sight of him about then, as he dived through the recreational ground – none of the kids was actually harmed, and the education people have sent counsellors – and then into the spruce plantation beyond. It runs 3 to 4 miles down through the valley, as you'll recall.

Several people have heard him crashing about, and we hear him trumpeting occasionally, although we think he only comes out to graze at night.

Seeing as Derek never formally handed over custody to me, I'm disinclined to accept responsibility for Hercules, and I have not, repeat *not*, reported an 'on movement'. The hire fee bill, which arrived in the relief post van today, is one I'm unlikely to be paying anytime soon. If it's of any interest, the grid reference of the entrance into the forestry is SX 652 695. Do let me know when you're planning to come and remove Hercules, as the Parish Council intend to sell tickets to view the spectacle from Bert's ridge fields opposite.

I beg to remain, etc etc
Ernest Buttcuss
(passport enclosed)

Cows vs ponies

We gathered the main bunch of Galloways last week, with the vague intention of sticking some metalwork in the winter calves' lugholes (and possibly even informing the government that we'd done so). As we got into the narrows at the foot of the valley, one of the Dartmoor mares that had tagged along hoping for a mouthful of hay from the bait bale turned to sock a week-old calf that she considered was in her way. The calf's mother, a solid and rotund dun belt, saw it coming, and was at the pony in a flash, head down, bellowing. The mare wasn't having a bit of it, and let go with both barrels at the cow. The latter sidestepped and pushed in again, bawling all the more. The mare had to realign to have another go, with the cow deftly making sure she was always between the pony and the calf. This went on for some minutes, until the cow was joined by another newly calved bellowing Beltie, and turned the tables. The mare fled. It was quite a spectacle.

Two things caught my attention. Firstly, the cow who charged in to help was the only sister I have to the first, both having come up from Bodmin in 2001. Secondly, once back in the yard, as I subsequently grabbed each of the 18 bawling calves in turn to tag and ring them, not one cow raised her voice at me. One or two came up real close – handy for reading a faded metal tag – but none really threatened me. I have no explanation for this at all.

I'm not going to admit to having omitted to pick up a couple of the mad black 'Doreens' when we went out for the cows originally. One of these cows – that I absolutely *did not* leave behind with untagged calves – had her eyes out on stalks, and went for me for just looking at her over the wall.

Obviously, if an inspector should visit I will happily pass him the pliers, saying 'She's over there guv, help yerself'! (When asked, upon the discovery of such a crime, what steps I intend to take, the answer can only be, all together now…'Very long ones indeed, sir'.)

The author trying to comply with regulations, and a cow called Doreen

Another bit of Galloway cattle lore for you. Arriving to feed the Galloways after a very wet night I will sometimes find them on the wrong side of 50 feet of raging river. Somehow the cows judge when it's feasible to cross, and I have to sit and watch the baby calves swim alongside. The cows won't cross once the water gets past a certain depth, and on the very odd occasion when a yearling or two ignore the older cows, they soon learn the error of their ways. This is all a bit heart-stopping so I tend to look the other way but, strangely, we virtually never lose animals in this fashion.

Eighteen months ago, I did the uncomfortable sums – with no headage payments, and costing my own labour – and figured I was about to lose 20 grand by keeping about 100 suckler cows in the coming year. Some of my colleagues were astonished, and smugly suggested I was some kind of idiot. Funny thing is, now EBLEX have done some maths using the self-same formula, it appears I'm one of the top performers in the country! Keeping my losses to £200 a cow seems to have been a result. (It should be observed that some of my aforementioned colleagues have since snuck back and whispered that their figures are worse. Much worse.)

🦋

It may have escaped your attention, but another Brit was been selected to go into space recently. This particular Anglonaut was suited and booted to go up and rewire the knackered old space station – a kind of high-tech cosmic Skoda. We know (and I suspect you're with me here…) that he clambered through the hatch, put his hands on his hips and sucked his teeth for a minute, and after a sharp intake of breath shook his head and said, 'You've had some right old cowboys in here, chief. This is gonna cost you.' (On the subject of things vaguely Russian, did I read that some bloke was recently poisoned with radioactive Palaminonium? What's that then, glow-in-the-dark particles of a mustard coloured 'oss?)

And finally, back on terra firma, I heard that the Queen has been kind enough to meet and greet a native American, to do a bit of posh hand-shaking and saying, 'How frightfully sorry we are that we nicked your country.' Well, I noticed something that I rather suspect the palace didn't. The Indian was apparently named 'Two Dogs'. We know a joke about that name, don't we boys and girls. I don't suppose anyone at the palace could admit to knowing such coarse stories, which would be how it slipped below the radar. No, let's be charitable – perhaps he really is called Two Dogs.

Bill and Ben the Flowerpot Men

A residual reminder of the desperately wet July last year has been having to use up the stinky bales of silage we wrapped that month. Those of you who've walked this stony road will know only too well the delights we're enjoying now.

Luckily, I suppose, only two days' work was really in the 'rank vinegar' category, equating to about 200 bales. Each one of these soggy dumplings has to be unwrapped, and unstrung, prior to feeding. It doesn't matter how careful you are, how many layers of waterproof clothing you don, how carefully you rub a bit of washing-up liquid into your hands before you start in the morning… you're still gonna stink of the blinking stuff at the end of the day.

The effluvia will linger, causing heads to turn and noses to wrinkle wherever you travel. The only escape is to visit with other livestock farmers who'll be sympathetic, if not actually likewise afflicted. Even then, they'll hardly want to concentrate the problem.

Ironically the cows are just as happy scoffing this pickled goo as they are the sweetest haylage, baled when it was only a breath of wind away from best hay. They seem to be doing reasonably OK on it. Even the Cheviot ewes that are sharing with some South Devon cows are eating it. (Mystery to me, pal.)

Not wanting to put young Joe off, I've been trying to handle the worst of it myself. There's a limit to what you can ask of a lad and anyway, come evenings, his thoughts must turn to whatever it is that interests a young man after work. Somehow I doubt if he'll be wanting this particular aftershave.

He has drawn the short straw with a couple of goes at tidying up manky sheep's feet (another carry-over from last summer's monsoon). These sessions in the sheep pens leave him forced to disrobe when he gets home, being banned from entering the house ponging so!

Leaving me to hold the fort, Alison has been trying to expose the kids to culture again (as opposed to them culturing something, which is different). To this end they've all been off to Londinium to take in the terracotta warriors, some of which China has very kindly lent to the British Museum for a stint. (Now I'm of the impression that this is a long drive just to see Bill and Ben the flowerpot men, but I'm firmly reminded I'm just a peasant, and that they are archaeological and cultural icons.)

Alison has in fact already been to China to see some of these things, just as some students thought they'd try traffic control with some tanks in Tiananmen Square. You might recall seeing them on the news at the time. Not a holiday Alison will soon forget! (Mind, while on the more recent trip, 'er had forgotten what her husband smelt like, and is now complaining.)

Some of you may have noticed a tide of suggestions that Jeremy Clarkson should, in fact, be running the country (usual 'time of writing' comments apply). In the first breath, I'll support this campaign, as I twigged long ago that Jezzer is a very much smarter man than his TV persona implies. You just can't be consistently that boorish without being very shrewd indeed, and his continued success has made him a national treasure… however, on reflection, what good would it do to give him a position of serious responsibility? He'd have to knuckle down and take the grown-up view, which would surely neuter the forthright outbursts we've come to expect. No Jezzer, you keep shooting from the hip.

Oh, and did you catch his chum Richard Hammond doing a show backalong, on *Evel Knievel* – shot in the States before old Evel 'jumped' into the next dimension? The show was fairly interesting in its exposure of what happens to an ex-media darling showman, who has somehow – miraculously in this case – managed to make it through to old age and natural infirmity.

But the real story was watching Hamster's own personal struggle with the image being reflected in front of him. Here was an old man who used to go off doing insane motorised stunts in the eye of the camera, blithely putting his loved ones through all kinds of hell. There was scarcely a mention of the comparisons to which both viewer and presenter must be drawn, but they are nonetheless written across the screen in pretty big letters.

This was, I suspect, a very sobering experience for Richard Hammond, and a striking piece of telly if you cared to notice the sub-text.

Ah, I have to briefly review a couple of recent comments… the smartest marked calf I was crowing about in the pre-Chrimbo batch promptly went down with the squits, terminally. Blinking typical isn't it? I could've volunteered half a dozen I'd sooner have lost, and really should know better than to have opened my extra-large mouth in the first place.

Oh, and another local tells me he's been under the knife… this one apparently to have a hip 'resurfaced'. Was this resurfacing achieved, I asked, by a transit load of swarthy lads with a pile of chippings, and a bubbling cauldron of bitumen? Were they working in the area 'Guv', and had some materials left over?

Hey ho: I'm off to feed some more silage, at arms' length.

Computer games and Git's departure

I'm currently grappling with bunny-hugger concerns about the safeguarding of the wet peat soils and wildlife about me, when ironically, in just a few years, or decades, my successor will probably be doing his or her utmost to get past the peat, and farm harder than ever.

It seems unlikely now doesn't it, but unless war, famine* or pestilence wipes billions (yes, billions) of mouths from the UN's predictions we are going to have to scalp this world's surface like locusts. In just a generation, we're going to gut the planet's resources like a fish.

*We seem to be incapable of viewing images of starving humans, struggling to stay alive in landscapes demonstrably unable to support them, without our hand-wringing consciences prompting us to try and support these hungry souls.

The usual response is one of two immediate options. Send food, or transport the hungry mouths down the road to where there's been better weather this season. Neither option will make things any better next year. Pretty far from it, in fact. And yet the third option is completely untouchable. ('Look away now if you don't want to know the score.')

I suppose if you can't stomach the brutal realities, you could try sending education and contraception. But I can't see that just sending grub is the answer.

I'd better move on, lest the hate mail engulfs us.

Meanwhile, I must apologise. I had thought of the most hilarious gag utilising a recent addition to 'youth speak'… the 'must have' computer-game gadget, the Wii, but it's gone again, and I forgot to make a note at the time.

This gag doubtless featured a sorry little wordplay: Wii-ding perhaps, or Wii-ping, or possibly just Wii-ing. Look, you just make up your own until it comes back to me.

And on the subject of computer games… Alison has been much involved in helping set up a farming computer game. Obviously, at trough time, the lads and I have been obliged to help her with this. We suggest there could be a space-invader-type game, where the player has to try and field runaway lambs as they march down the screen. Or a little Professor Winston lookalike could march round, scoring points for all the ramblers he sets the dogs on, or lame sheep he curses. Every rep he nudges into the waist-deep slurry puddle could be points; he could hide in a variety of places from the bank manager/HSE or cross-compliance inspector/mother-in-law/berserk bull. The list is pretty much endless (and probably rather more fun than the actual game will be).

It is with great regret that I have to report on the passing of top Scotch tup 'Git'. He was born in 2001, slipping into the fog with his mother and a score of aunties. Through that empty summer, Tom and I could see them brazenly grazing across a supposedly clear newtake. We kept well clear until September, when the heat seemed to have died down, and slipped out with the dogs to retrieve them – it really was time to get the wool off their backs. Given the flock's history these few ewes were beyond price to me, and amongst them was an outstanding strapper of a tup lamb. Only one thing to do with him, wasn't there?

Git in his prime

Wintering on a farm full of grass, he soon grew into everything I'd have wished. Sadly, however, his behaviour let him down. Misunderstanding my instructions, he resolved to impregnate every sheep in the parish, Scotch or otherwise.

He'd jump a five-bar gate like a stag, and crash at anything higher until he broke it.

He left me with a flock of his many daughters, and after I was first to set a hand on him at six months, I was also then the last. He went mad in the dip this time round, threw his head back, and drowned before I could pull him out. I rarely need an excuse to raise a dram, but he's been as good a reason as I shall have.

Speaking of dipping, for many months I've had a niggling injury to my hand, sustained in the dip pen. Just as it has gone away, and stopped grizzling, up steps some pillock to give me one of those bone-crunching handshakes that say how tough he thinks he is. Initially I warned off likely looking assailants, but you can only do that for so long. Now I just keep my hands in my pockets when approached by such folks.

Didn't Charrière say that a man's handshake should be firm, but without too much effort, neither like a show-off, nor the limp handshake of a ponce? (I don't know if I'm allowed to use that word nowadays – the PC inspectors will be wagging their – unbruised – fingers at me).

Before leaving this topic: as a lad with no grasp of the niceties of polite society, I asked, 'Should I shake a lady's hand, Dad?' The advice given – to which I've always adhered – was… 'Only when she offers it, boyo.'

SPRING 2008

Egil Skallgrimson

I have an admission. Whilst trucking about in the Land Rover I've found myself flinching, as I catch a glimpse of something just in my field of vision. Close examination has revealed that what seemed to be a large bird flitting away just over the hedge is in fact a couple of runaway eyebrow hairs, just tickling my peripheral vision.

Yes friends, I've reached that moment in a man's life when he realises that his eyebrows are about to become those whiskery caterpillars that adorned the aged men of his youth.

Reflecting that some urban men don't wear these badges of experience and wisdom caused me to realise that they must practise eyebrow topiary* of some kind. Now there's strange!

That balding medieval Icelander 'Egil' comes to mind. He could, apparently, perform tricks with his eyebrows (one would crawl down his cheek, whilst the other migrated back over his forehead).

Aside from being a farmer of some note, and a poet of international repute, Egil also had a phenomenally bad temper, and a propensity for falling out with authority, bull wrestling and generally leaving an axe in your forehead if you looked at him in a funny way.

I realise we'd better move on, before you all start making unkind comparisons.

*Back to the eyebrows and personal grooming. Do you think I'd be allowed to employ some nice young Polish or Lithuanian girl to undertake such tasks? Possibly not, eh? (I recall that old Egil got in a fair old ding-dong whilst on a 'boating trip' to that end of the Baltic, but you'll just have to go and read about that for yourself.)

Don't you just love the continuing concept of the farmer being able to turn his hand to anything? And indeed, many of them can. Why, I myself can function as a very mediocre carpenter, a half-arsed accountant, an unqualified and ill-advised vet, a positively useless mechanical fitter, a downright dangerous tree feller, an overly eager but inept plant operator, a spectacularly incompetent auto-first-aid operative, a famously poor welder, a renowned public relations expert ('Get orf my land, or I'll set the dogs on 'ee!') and, best of all, a pretty useless livestock farmer! I would naturally hesitate to suggest that any of my peers carry similar qualifications.

Despite all this, have you noticed that when the excrement strikes the air circulator, everyone will turn to us? Wherever there is a crisis, whatever the nature, modern man still has to turn to the local peasant.

Floods left you stranded in your car? Don't worry, a farmer will soon chug along on his tractor and rescue you.

Snowdrift caught hold of the school bus? Same farmer will trundle up and tug 'em out with his tractor.

There are the contemporary political versions... Made some ill-advised world stage promises regarding the state of yer SSSIs? Don't flap; the peasants will come to the rescue!

And the historic... Was a Nazi world-domination plan going to starve you into submission? Don't fret Maister, the same old farmer, or p'haps his Dad, will just mosey along and plough up some grassland for spuds.

And the very historic, I suppose... Want some time off to invent civilisation? Give us a couple of hours, Guv, and one of us will be along with a domesticated ox to discover ploughing and cereal farming, and leave everyone else to have a bit of spare time to devise the civil service, taxation and organised religion.

And looking forward... Global population in an uncontrolled upward spiral? Billions heading for conflict or starvation? Now, who will they ask?

I love it. Unqualified bodging yokels were, and remain, the foundation of the modern world, yet remain pretty much invisible (until you're stuck in the proverbial snowdrift, that is).

I'm reminded of a pal of mine who, as a young man, was on shift work when the storm of January 1990 whooshed through, flattening half the trees in this end of the country. Being of a rural bent, and on his 'week off', he phoned the council's highways department and offered his services ('Have Husqvarna, will travel'). This was in a somewhat different era, and the reply was 'Thanks son, you're hired. Here's a list of roads blocked. Get on with it, and send us the bill.'

My pal admits (albeit much later and in a very quiet voice) that he was quite a way down the job sheet before he came to a tree that hadn't already been heaved out over into the next-door field because it was in the way of a milk tanker or a lorry load of fat cattle waiting to go. He omitted to mention this 'agricultural assistance' when submitting his bill.

I suppose his luck wasn't always thus. Another time, the same lad accompanied a few of us out onto a Hebridean island in search of cheap Scotch ewe lambs (at least that was the excuse given for the trip).

History doesn't relate how many ewe lambs were to be found, but records all too clearly how a pair of blue-and-white collie pups were secured, and how on our last night our young pal won a bottle of the local malt at a ceilidh (and felt obliged to do his best by the prize). He and the collie pups had to travel in the back of a hire car the next day, after a somewhat turbulent ferry crossing, and were, all three, 'unwell' for some hundreds of miles.

I might recall a number of other incidents occurring on such trips – the search for supplies of healthy Scotch ewe lambs being somewhat secondary to the consumption of significant volumes of obscure malts – were it not for the fact that the protagonists are now such pillars of the community (unmarked envelopes full of used tenners being the surest way to maintain this amnesia).

I s'pose there's some farming news as well, but I'm out of time so you can make it up yourselves.

Ponies vs cows

I do enjoy being right in amongst the cows – whom I love deeply, their proximity bringing peace to my soul – but why do they have to target my toes? If I want to push an old girl aside, there is a good chance that once a week one of these dear ladies will plant her hoof directly onto my toes, usually pivoting as she does. If you've enjoyed this experience you'll know your reaction is to push her away, making a noise as you do so. This will certainly speed her out of the way. Sadly it will also cause her to transfer all her weight onto your pinkie to do so. Ow!

By contrast, being in amongst a bunch of Dartmoor ponies (which I detest and loath, wretched kicking biting bad-tempered creatures that they are) is a quite different experience.

Being pretty much feral, when you're five feet away from the back end they'll surely want to spring their rumps into the air, ready to let you have both barrels. But once you're right in

The author with some of his friends

amongst them, backside to backside, you're perfectly safe. Your toes will rarely get squashed, and they don't kick sideways like a flighty bullock might. They are, I suppose, rather more wont to bite than cows, but you can't have everything.

The end of winter seemed to have just about arrived when the wet and cold returned. You know it's bad when there's a couple of a mallard swimming beside the round feeder in the morning.

I realise I haven't been giving the beauro-crap mountain my full attention. It has certainly been piling up as much as ever, so I'll address this omission by looking at my dip disposal licence.

I'm joyfully paying some government department £3 a week to be permitted to spread the contents of the sheep dip onto my own fields. Quite apart from resenting parting with any of my coin at all, I rather begrudge paying this particular bill, as the only people directly affected by any potential groundwater issues are my immediate family and I.

In fact, why the whole hoo-ha about the disposal of used OP dips? When I went and took my dipping test (after a lifetime of happily dipping sheep without having sat such a test) I was given to understand – always had understood, in fact – that the dip mixture is little better than useless after the first day, as all the little molecules of chemical lock themselves to the poop bobbing about the water. The old OPs are rendered quite ineffective.

Oh? In that case brother, why is there the fuss about spreading the stuff across the field?

I must truly be a simpleton, now I come to think about it, because I also note that whilst I can't eat my sheep for a month or so after dipping, they seem to be free of nasty itches for 10 to 12 weeks. Obviously there's something I'm missing there as well.

Sorry, another thought occurs. Being a well-behaved chap, and having taken my dipping test so I can purchase OP sheep dip, I remain perplexed that anyone can go along and buy the same chemicals, for 'different applications', with absolutely no questions asked at all. Funny old world, isn't it.

These matters have been uppermost in my mind as I've had to wash some of the sheep again, just before lambing. The itch appeared right in the middle of the farm, late in February. Seeing as everything here was carefully washed in November, in a supposedly Dartmoor-wide co-ordinated attack, that galled me somewhat.

One or two vigilant colleagues and I are now quietly discussing how we broach the topic with the mongrels who don't seem to give a damn (current favourite is with the aid of heavy cudgels).

I long ago learned to treat the itch in sheep with the utmost caution, the old men around me in my youth being very direct in their opinions on the matter. It'll now be a blinking miracle if we're not going to have to co-ordinate an extra dipping session at shearing.

Ironically, I hear that it is widely expected that all my neighbours and I are going to queue up to vaccinate our ewes against some new foreign lurgy as well! I'm sorry to say that I harbour the gravest reservations about that plan, old man.

Hey, you know when the workload is a bit heavy, and fetching in some more firewood is a chore you could do without… well, my eye keeps on falling on a piece of bog oak I've got propped inside the back door. The Galloways rubbed it out of a peat bank backalong, whilst scratching their shaggy heads. Being as it grew just up the valley, maybe a couple of thousand years ago – much further up than oaks currently grow, I should add – it seems pretty precious. Ostensibly it's awaiting some skilled artisan turning it into a trinket to keep around the house, but

I'm now worried a late spring chilly evening will see it gone up in smoke!

It reminds me of Solzhenitsyn's story about the discovery of a fantastically preserved woolly mammoth, lying frozen in the Siberian permafrost. The discovery was made by some of Stalin's 'unwanted' comrades, sent to Siberia to disappear (their crimes typically being in the 'looking at me in a funny way' category). Elation in the scientific community on news of the discovery soon turned to confusion however, when it fast became clear that the starving 'Zeks' who found this treasure had straight away set to and eaten it. All of it.

Livestock transit tests

With some official deadline looming, we all hurriedly trucked off to take our transport test recently – all credit to NFU for organising this test. It was a 60-mile round trip at a busy time of year, but rules is rules. We all passed – most of the answers being blinking obvious – and hurried on our way home again.

Unfortunately, homecoming revealed a South Devon cow, calved, prolapsed, with a fair-sized bull calf. Both lying quite dead, in the cold cold rain. Nowt was happening before we left, but they were dead as dogs' doings before we got back.

Now I've been around the transporting of livestock all my life, having put in time as both lorry driver and market drover as a youth. I've loaded and seen loaded many many thousands of cattle, and I never recall injuring a cow more than the odd scrape and scratch. Going to take a test on the subject then cost me a cow I was quite fond of.

Irony George. Irony.

Whilst trying to work out how to keep related heifers and bulls apart, my pal Colin and I came to the conclusion that, um... 'very close' breeding, like blood sports, can't be all bad. After all, they've always been the preserve of both extreme ends of society!

When it works you call it 'line breeding', when it doesn't it's 'in-breeding'. (Colin then went on to share a humorous story about chickens, which I'm afraid I am absolutely not going to share with you polite folks.)

Ere! I've been reading some science stuff again, and guess what? Quite a developed academic area of study is considering how 'civilisation' will cope with fairly modest upsets in various supply chains (specifically food and power in the paper). It may tickle you to hear that these boffins (in several worthy institutes) have realised that as our global community becomes increasingly complex and interdependent, the house of cards becomes correspondingly unstable.

Even a flu pandemic – which we can be sure will turn up again at some point – will tip our supply logistics into a tailspin. Never mind fatalities, just the absences from the work place will bring down entire supply and power systems.

See how a handful of striking Scottish oil refinery staff could impact the country recently? A widely reached conclusion has been that keeping no 'slack' is courting disaster. Where ancient societies judged their security on how many granaries they kept full, modern government and business has been preoccupied with maintaining the very minimum of reserves, whilst complicating and stretching our lines of communication and commerce.

Now factor in the tightening food supply, even in 'fair weather', and I can see why these professor types are a little agitated.

❧

Look, I don't want you to run away with the idea that I'm enamoured of the TV survival specialists… pretty far from it as it goes.

My lovely wife and I thought for a long time that the one who looks like a slightly chubby overgrown Boy Scout, who's always cooking some root or leaf, and saying 'Mmm, delicious' was in fact doing a comedy show. But apparently he's quite earnest, and lots of armchair dwellers think he's the bee's whatsit.

Does it never occur to them that living on twigs and half-cooked weeds tends to leave you looking a bit… how can I put this delicately… thinner? And when he's conversing with the native chieftain, through a translator, we all know the native is really saying 'Him big fella, him feed whole tribe this week. Wife number 5, where big cauldron got to?' (He even lights the fire for them!)

Another one, who at least looks lean and tough (no name, no pack drill), supposedly goes off into some remote place, trekking back to civilisation with the aid of nothing more than a pocket knife and his teeth, living off slugs and dew. But funnily enough, as he scrambles up some cliff edge, the camera crew is already there waiting for him. We sussed him for a fraud straight off. Now he's had to admit that he does in fact retire to a hotel for the evening when filming's done.

No, not for me, old boy.

In a different league, however, is that Bruce Parry.

He's the disarming one who goes off to live with some tribe of natives while somehow managing not to be the condescending white man. He ends up struggling like hell not to marry the chief's daughter or become blood brothers with the shaman. He too will eat all kinds of suspect stuff, but ruefully admits it's awful (then has to excuse himself while he goes off for a chunder).

There is something self-effacing and integral about old Bruce. I suspect you could, as they used to say, go tiger hunting with him. The point being that when life's long grasses start rustling, and you discover your rifle is jammed, you'll be wanting someone at your side whose gun bloody well hasn't jammed and, more pointedly, is still beside you. Certain other individuals would either start to blub, and be found in a spreading steaming pool, or leave an empty space, with a few leaves see-sawing slowly to the ground. Bruce strikes me as the kind of bloke who would be there.

His travels have very evidently shown him much of human nature, and I suspect he's gained a very good grip on the world. By his own admission, he's subsequently asked the deepest questions of himself. Go for high office Bruce, you've got my vote.

And finally, for those of you who, like me, have been spending time wrestling cattle to attach earrings and detach unwanted appendages, I have something to share. The archaeological record of Neanderthal skeletons shows they were almost always very banged around in life. They usually have evidence of various broken limbs, traumatic amputations and the like.

Now some clever scientist has tried a direct comparison with injuries in modern professions.

And who turns out to have similar trauma patterns? Competitive rodeo riders as it happens have a surprisingly, even uncannily, similar pattern of limb fractures. They wrestle bullocks for fun as well, don't they?

Blue tongue

Yes, yes: I have been sticking some blue tongue vaccine in the cattle, as and when I come within an arm's length of them. Don't nag so. And what a pain in the stern it's been as well. The two yearlings which skipped away over the brow, tails in the air, were firmly told they could soddin' well get the pox.

Shearing is upon us (although Uncle T. has understandably left it to Dave this summer), and handling the sheep will involve a whole lot more vaccine.

The bulls are at it, and by the time you lot get this I s'pose I'll have a mower out. Fingers crossed.

Now I had written a couple of paragraphs on how the world is shaping up, but it's all a bit old hat now, since someone has at last whispered in Gordon's ear that things might not be quite so peachy after all (we always knew, didn't we, that old Tony was going to cling to the steering wheel right up 'til he could see the precipice, and then jump out the door shouting 'Your turn now Gordy!'). So I had to start again.

On the subject of number crunching in the new world order (which I was, in the deleted stuff) I believe I'm not alone in noticing that lamb and beef prices haven't kept in front of input prices.

I'm very much afraid we won't be putting our collective pedal to the metal just yet. In any case, there are already bleating voices that if farmers rush to increase production, they'll compromise biodiversity *et al.*

This concern seems pretty extraneous to a bloke looking into some hundreds of acres of boulder-strewn bracken and gorse, too steep or wet to drive over. The clearing of this ground to raise a few more lambs is completely uneconomic, and I only do battle with it on general principles. Oh, alright then, I'll try not to step on any caterpillars.

I have at least been getting out a bit. Last week we all trucked on down to civilised parts for a night out.

Firstly, we had called in to see friend Trevor Dawe to secure a very solid Angus bull, for my eldest's pedigree Angus ladies (she now needs to re-home a smart yearling of our own breeding, all paper-worked up, details on request).

Next up we trundled across the valley for Alice and Brian's

annual barbie. This event can only occur once the first cut is in the clamp, so the assembled reprobates can slide gracefully to the horizontal in the field behind the yard.

A sure sign of the times was when, as shadows lengthened and the old faces started rolling in, they arrived not on bikes with tents and bedrolls lashed to the rack but in 4x4s full of kids, pulling caravans. Long-term resident guitarist Fred turned up in his new shiny campervan, no less.

It was rather disquieting to witness grown-up ex-tear-arses earnestly comparing the merits of various caravans (Nigel did try to rekindle things tearing around on a trike, but it didn't seem the same somehow). I felt obliged to keep standards up by bivouacking my lot on Galloway hide rugs, in a wobbly tent and under a satisfyingly bodged tarp strung from the back of the Discovery.

Nigel on the trike

And so to the job in hand. Our hosts had kindly provided masses of soft padded things for the kids to climb on and fall off, and a couple of terrifying rope swings (best not to watch I find) in the barn next door. This allowed the rest of us to step aboard the old lager-fuelled time machine. Marvellous fun. Sure enough, we were soon all 21 again, and embarrassing the kids with some spectacular 'Dad-dancing'. A load of half-cut Eastern European builders had snuck in, and were also going well. (Mind, if this is the 'Pole dancing' I keep hearing about you can keep it mate.)

I'm not going to admit that, as the evening went on, Nige and I might've heckled the band just a touch. But I ask you: if Fred could sing a witty ditty titled 'The Limp Percy Blues' so happily 25 years ago, why on earth would he feel a bit tetchy about performing it now? (Remind me to ask Mrs Fred if there is some reason for this!)

Thanks Alice and Brian: it was great, and I'm dreadfully sorry if my behaviour let me down again. See you next year (boldly assuming we're allowed back).

Further family outings have included a trip up into Gloucester. Chiefly, we were off to visit to a very posh garden near Tetbury (yes, that one, and very nice it is and all) but we also took a picnic in Westonbirt Arboretum. I wasn't able to get the Husqvarna through security, and the kids and I couldn't quite uproot this particular beanpole (overleaf).

I did resolve something that had been bothering me since my last visit. How on earth could such thin Cotswold limestone soil grow such magnificent oak timber? So I scooped up a handful of molehill dirt in the parkland this time, and found it an unexpectedly rich sandy stuff. Under the trees 100 years of leaf mould had turned it a fantastic crumbly black.

But I was still puzzled. Where had it come from? The head gardener at the posh garden (a VIG?) was able to give me the answer. Long ago there was a huge lake lying across what would become that part of the Cotswolds, and the soil under much of both properties includes four feet of prehistoric alluvial. Ah: that explains that then.

Finally, I'm reminded to lead you gently to the 'Dartmoor farmer' computer game, which is now live. My beloved had, you might recall, all sorts of fun helping put it together, and you might have some fun trying it out. Here's the link: www.dartmoor-npa.gov.uk/fz-interactives

The chooks strike back

Lots of wildlife goings-on... just like *Springwatch* here mate. There's a wren has to hop down with a mouth full of wrigglies whenever I'm carrying stuff out from the mill, waiting for me to get away from her nest. Several pairs of blackbirds, masses of robins, a few wagtails, and a pair of redstart have all raised clutches around the yard, along with the droves of swallows.

Then whilst we were looking at some cows out on the Forest last week, the boy and I found a pond absolutely heaving with newts! (I would admit that this pond was the result of a blocked drainage ditch, but that would only encourage the 're-wilding' lunatics, wouldn't it?*)

Ah! The boy and his fowls. He's become very keen on poultry, and has taken over feeding duties for some of Alison's semi-feral banties. This spring saw an early clutch successfully reared in the pen by the back door. They too have been attracting wildlife. Last week a small hawk-type raptor found its way into the cage, and set off a fair cacophony at 6am. John came rushing in at 6.10 to tell us a hawk was trying to eat his chickens. In fact, the hawk was desperately trying to escape from the pen, as a posse of beady-eyed velociraptors huddled together in a circle, discussing in a low twittering whether they should go on the offensive.

Don't laugh. The bird was lucky it hadn't got in with last year's clutch. They attacked and ate several songbirds that visited them, leaving only the beaks! Anyway Alison let this one out, although I bet the little chap won't be back very soon.

I see the bunny huggers in a new light in the face of emerging food supply news. By all means bother me about saving some more

Left Tidy oak stick at Westonbirt
Right Hawk in with chooks

newts, but only if you're prepared to point out which people you want to go hungry. If I fail to rear a little Scotch lamb on that patch of wet, or in amongst this brackeny bank, someone somewhere is going to go hungry. Sounds pretty unlikely, but that's the reality isn't it?

I would have said that the storm is pretty much upon us, and the timetable is much shorter than we thought. Come back Malthus, you needed to consider oil in your equation.

Seriously, I haven't looked very hard, but I expect that some professor type somewhere has used Malthusian theory, factoring society's reliance on oil to grow food, and come up with some numbers we're going to find very, very uncomfortable.

Ho-hum. I can't honestly say I care too much.

Anyway, I'd better get on and see if I can find a shearer and some BT vaccine. I've already got some sweaty sheep to hand.

Summer 2008

Illiterate farmers and Tolstoy

Childcare on Dartmoor: the kids with South Devon bull 'Ross'

I've been doing all the summer jobs you'd expect. Blue-tongue-jabbing stock, with injection guns that soon fail to deliver a full charge, and needles better suited to hooking trout from the stream. I've been fetching cows in for a liaison with the bulls, fetching yearlings back from wherever they've got out and gone to.

And, of course, I've been waiting on the weather. I'm not really late, at the time of blogging,* but would like to make a start now. I'm having a nasty feeling of *déjà vu* here.

Still at least some sheep are sheared.

A linguistic nicety. 'Blogging' isn't the same as 'dogging', and 'dogging' isn't the term it used to be. I'd advise a degree of care in the use of such terms.

Oh, and on linguistic matters I've a question for you. Why on earth is 'dyslexia' such a soddin' difficult word to spell? Seems doubly cruel, doesn't it? My pal Sascha and I have decided we are going to replace the word 'dyslexia' with something much more phonetic. ('Ob' is the current favourite, but we're civilised men, and will happily take better suggestions.)

I'm not going to venture into the murky territory of all the different names currently in circulation for 'not learning to read'. I readily concede that I'm just a grumpy reactionary old peasant, and that no one should be labelled 'not very bright' any more. What is it they have? 'Special needs'. Right.

Mind, in my rose-tinted past, lads who couldn't quite get the hang of their letters usually got by quite well, oft becoming perfectly capable craftsmen. Why, now I come to think of it, I can think of some who became very proficient indeed at their work. One or two who topped their professions, whose names you would recognise, but who still couldn't make their way to the bottom of the page. (And about whom you'd think I could write whatever I liked. I tend not to, on the grounds that whilst they might not be able to read, they may very well be able to pay someone else to do so on their behalf. And someone else again to come round and thump me.)

And while we're navigating these choppy waters… It's long been observed that the government have now made the position of an illiterate farmer pretty much untenable, which seems pretty stupid, thinking of all the very competent stockmen I've known who were never able to get the hang of Tolstoy.

OK, a joke for you. The man from the work and pensions department turns up to check out a farmer's employment practices.

'I'd like to know how many you employ, their working terms and conditions, and how much they're paid,' he announced officiously.

'Werrll,' said the old farmer, 'there's the cowman. He works eight hours a day, five days a week, some of it indoors. He has holiday pay, time off, and takes 'ome about £300 a week, with yon cottage thrown in. Then there's the maid who helps with the sheep. She works six days a week, nine hours a day, out in all weathers and I let her have a week or two off when the lambs are all sold. 'Er earns £250 a week, and 'as full board an' lodging in the farmhouse.

'Lastly there's the half-wit. He works seven days a week, 52 weeks of the year. He doesn't actually get holiday pay, or sick pay, but that don't matter, cos the idiot's never off. He does all the filthiest jobs, and earns about £20 a week, but 'ee does get him a gallon of cider most every Saturday night. Oh, and he gets to sleep with my wife occasionally.'

'Good grief! That's awful,' exclaims the inspector. 'He is the employee I need to see. Where is he right now?'

'Talking to you, pal.'

Cornish directions

In between the piddling showers we have made a good dent in the hay harvest. So far it's involved a lot of wrap again. Out of 50 acres cut, only 50 round bales have been deemed dry enough to be left unwrapped. Still, think how much shed space I'll start the winter with.

Calamities have mostly centred on the blood spilled during rows about who gets to drive which tractor. The plum choices are the one with the air-con, or the one with functional radio. Less desirable is the old Deere whose linkage is operated by a mole wrench beside the driver's right boot, and with 'ambient through flow air-con' and 'karaoke radio'. Still, it pulled out of the nettles and worked well again, despite being a good bit older than its lucky operator!

Domestically I'm enjoying this parenting business, but doesn't it bring its own complications?

Uncle T. shows Agnes how to earn pocket money

There's the ongoing subject of when should be 'bedtime' (still set early, despite threats of revolt. And no, I'm not going to say my children are revolting. You know that already!).

Then there's the bizarre concept of something called 'pocket money'. This is the alleged gift, by some parents, of hard coin of the realm, in exchange for – as I understand it – absolutely no goods or services whatsoever. Not round here it blinking well isn't. If they run errands, fetch the logs in, feed the chickens, help Mother round the house, and stand to attention when I get in at the end of the day, I might consider not clouting them sharply around the ear holes!

I am of course joking. The boy is generally keen to help, and already very handy. I realise I'm starting to plan jobs around when he's home. The girls are now presenting cooked items that can be eaten without trepidation! All three can proficiently work the bale wrapper, roll wool, paint sheep, and stand in a gap.

In return, they want for nothing that they actually need, and, if they keep their sights low, little that they desire.

Anyway, the next hurdle is mobile phones. Eldest is about to go up a school, and I'm reliably informed that this is the point when they should be given their own phone. Ha! Not on my watch, kiddo. It comes to my attention that some of the primary school kids already have these gadgets, which I regard as a tax on the gullible.* I do recognise that I'm lagging some decades behind the rest of the world, but I'm still digging my heels in, fighting a rearguard action.

*I did get some black looks whilst on holiday in Scotland last year. Whilst queuing in a chip shop, my youngest asked what the machine with the flashing lights and buzzers was – it was the techno equivalent of a one-armed bandit – and I replied, in a loud voice, that it was a tax-collecting machine, for taking extra tax from STUPID people. This tax is voluntary, I explained, and we don't have to pay it, because we're not that STUPID.

The proprietor, and local clientele, weren't impressed. In fact, both looked positively annoyed.

Ah. Now, 'directions'.

Don't ask for directions when visiting the far west. You'll only get told, 'You know that turning left by the post-box? Well don't take that one. Go out past where Bill's old dairy used to be, then turn off where the big ash blew over last year, an' don't go as far as where the school bus crashed, just stop by the drain that overflows come Christmas.'

Of course, the exchange sometimes goes the other way. 'I say George, is this the way to Widecombe?' (posh voice emanating from new sports car). 'Ow d'you know my name's Garge?' replies flat-capped man, looking up from whatever he's shovelling beside the road. 'Why, I guessed old chap.' 'Well,' says flat cap, returning to his task, 'You can guess yer bleddy way to Widecombe.'

Another variation, from my youth, was the cosmic 'bull swap run' west, for Mary the bull hire lady. You'd start with two or three beefy boys on board to deliver, and as many to pick up and take somewhere else, and yet more to come home for a rest. (It is widely recognised that these chaps live a deeply contented life, and you rarely have to coax a hire bull up the ramp!) The day's instruction would include very few phone numbers, and no addresses. You would however have a collection of cryptic clues. A typical run might include… 'The first Hereford goes to the chap behind Trebinthere Aerodrome. His brother at Trelost is having the other one, so ask when you get to the first. The Angus is going to the chap that had that Charolais last year down by the estuary. You remember. He knows where you've got to pick up the Maine Anjou that's got to come back to the place with the narrow gate before Camelbridge. Don't forget to go back for the Sim that that chap's cousin wanted gone last month, it's got to go to the place with the big silo that you can see from the A30. Oh, and if you've got time, ask in the post office in St Mewling if the postman's uncle has finished with that Limo yet.'

And in passing, I should like to know, if you can hardly move for seagulls around the coast… inland as well even… and they'll nick your fish and chips for tuppence, why on earth are they so protected? (They are indeed protected I'm told.) I would like to think that if one should swoop down and grab your takeaway, you should be allowed to immediately substitute it for fresh raw gull!

Bullocks calving, and dancing in the rain!

I won't talk about the weather. If it's got better then it'll all be a memory, and if it ain't... well, our not having sufficient grass saved for my moth-eaten old cows is hardly the biggest problem the nation will have.

I'm not a religious man at all – I'd pray at the altar of Richard Dawkins, if it wasn't such a contradiction – but by golly, I can see how a man might turn to prayer.

🦋

Here! If I flush that big old steer out of the brambles down in the valley bottom, is he 'bush meat'?

🦋

When doing our annual 'mobile sawmilling demonstration' at the South West Woodfair I usually contrive some woody-type competition for visitors to our leaky gazebo. It might be 'guess the species of these sample planks' or, this year, 'guess the combined age of the pictured tree and lumberjack'.

The prize is a voucher for £20 worth of our products. This might be £20 towards a Land Rover load of firewood, or some beef or lamb. It might be the deposit on an oak beam, or £20 gets you quite a nice-looking block of my granite. It might even be a down payment towards a hide rug*, a pedigree Dartmoor pony, or a smart Galloway or South Devon heifer. We'll try our utmost to find something of interest.

Entrants are advised however, that if they have no use for local sustainable timber, and don't eat local beef or lamb, or utilise any of our products, the alternative prize might be a quantity of 'sound advice' from Mr Coaker.

*Oh, hide rugs. A couple of years ago, when he was up on the common checking his ewes, Farmer X was perplexed by my unusually colourful calves on the Galloways – by a borrowed Riggit bull. He scratched his head for a day or two, then, when we were next met exclaimed... 'Ere yer blighter, yer breedin' rugs aren't you!' Ne'er a truer word, said Farmer X.

Sadly, a slaughter man who ought to remain nameless has now shredded the hides of both the spectacular spotty steers I had ready. A solid black will peel as clean as you like, but these two, for whom I had paying customers waiting... didn't.

Meanwhile, speaking of hides, I've been told off for suggesting – in the NFU blog – that I'd like to peel a couple of DEFRA employees alive and tan their hides for my drumheads. (Specifically whichever *mongrels invented the lunacy of double-tagging and worse, double electro-tagging, hill sheep.) Well I'm unrepentant, and no doubt some of you will be contributing to my defence fund.*

Another annual jamboree we get involved in is the Riggit Galloway Cattle Society summer excursion, which has been and gone recently. This roving beano was Westcountry based this year. We enjoyed a rare sunny afternoon viewing my cattle on various hillsides. The beasts showed themselves perfectly, excepting a pair of South Devons who got to scrapping, and barged into a delegate's parked Land Rover. I'm sorry John, really really sorry...

Various further-travelled delegates were perplexed by my use of the description 'bullocks' in reference to any group of bovines, male, female, or mixed. I rarely think about this term, but between us we worked out that it is a Westcountry peculiarity, the rest of the English-speaking world using the term specifically in reference to castrated male cattle.

One visiting Riggit breeder is married to a retired Scottish vet who once, many years ago, did a bit of locum vetting in Devon. He was completely at sea when a customer phoned, and asked 'um to come quick', as 'ee 'ad a bullock bad with milk fever'. By the time another such local rung to say he was having trouble calving a 'bullock', the young vet was beginning to spot the pattern.

The second day of our get-together saw us heading further west for a farm visit to the estimable Mr Nankervis. Whilst he didn't share my luck with the weather – it absolutely chucked it down for much of the afternoon – Colin sure beats us all hands down for enthusiasm. He somehow managed to combine our visit with hosting a summer camp-out for the local rugby club (and no, Granny doesn't need to know what they got up to), and hosting his significant birthday party in a marquee in the garden – five years to the bus pass, Colin!

In between fetching and carrying vast trays of serious pasties and huge steaming vats of 'limpy curry', receiving guests from all over the country and worrying that everyone had everything they needed, Colin took us lot on a whirlwind tour of his collection of native cattle. I lost count at groups of 12 different breeds, with the obscurity prize going to his herd of Blue Albions.

The last group, of course, was to be the Riggits. Sadly, as they ambled up out of the bracken, out over some windswept West Penwith moor, the downpour intensified to monsoon levels. When a herd of Galloways turn tail and run for cover, you know the going's heavy.

We retreated to help celebrate Colin's birthday. Festivities continued long into the night, and by the time Alison and I were shoehorning tired kids back into the truck the monsoon had seeped under the marquee, and guests were donning their 'West Cornwall dancing pumps' (or Wellington boots, as the rest of us know them). Happy birthday Colin!

Ear notches and agaric toadstools

Movement forms.

Just about every time I move some stock I get a polite call from some desk jockey, advising me that I've filled the paperwork in wrong, again. (I've tried telling them I'm illiterate, but they won't buy it.)

Anyroad, one of my repeat offences is using out-of-date forms (there is some tiny change in the serial number, which makes the otherwise identical old forms completely obsolete). Recently these out-of-date forms have been taken straight from the pad sent from on high after a previous round of 'out-of-date' paperwork.

Hmm, that's interesting, as Alison is 100 percent sure she ditched the originals, and that the current batch must've been obsolete when they arrived.

I reckon I'll be obsolete soon enough, so I'm not overly vexed by this matter.

Ah! Now this must bring me to ear tags in hill sheep, and the looming lunacy of double-tagging and, worse, EID.

It is a centuries-old hill-farming tradition that each flock, on a given area of hill, will have its own ear-notch pattern. These marks aid sorting sheep on common land, and serve as the final arbiter as to exactly whose sheep is whose. Individual marks are passed down generations, over centuries – I use a mark unchanged from my Grandfather's entry in the local flock book of 1922 – each 'flock mark' generally staying with the leared/ hefted ewes on a farm, should the farmer move on.

Paint marks serve similar functions, but don't have quite the same security. After all, it's not too difficult to remove a sheep's wool, whereas removing its ears is a bit messier. (For obvious reasons, a heavy and deep ear-mark is oft regarded with heavy and deep suspicion.)

Marking the ewe lambs from outlying hill flocks can only be done once the stray sheep are carefully separated out. The correct sorting of ewes with their unmarked lambs is an annual task taken very seriously. Sloppy practice will lead to social ostracism… at best.

On Dartmoor, because we're grazing over such large tracts of rough (or possibly because we're a lot of cynical beggars) both cattle and ponies are often ear-marked as well, and branded, to boot. Hot-branding cattle is, I'm told, outlawed long since. (Obviously the cows I see so marked must simply be very, very old cows.)

Oh, I should warn you. Social services tend to frown if you ear-mark or brand the kids, however much you think it'll stop 'em getting lost in town.

Now, to get to the point, it strikes me as just a bit ironic that DEFRA are choosing to implement dual-tagging sheep, and even make silly noises about electro-tagging, on the most pointless of precepts*, when half the country's ewes are already indelibly identified to their farm of origin, voluntarily, using a system proven over centuries, and costing just about nowt.

Somehow it's just so *them*, isn't it?

Never forget, this stupid fixation with sheep IDs was sparked with the wholly unjustified idea that sheep are secretly harbouring some BSE-like ailment. Somehow, despite having admitted that some imbeciles were testing the 'wrong brains' for six months, government can't abandon all the plans subsequently set in motion.

As an afterthought, I've long been aware that the Lapps, or Sami, who herd reindeer in Scandinavia use an essentially identical system of ear-marking to distinguish whose reindeer are whose. The summer corralling of the herds to sort and mark the youngstock is in most respects exactly parallel to the sorting and handling of hill sheep here.

It occurs to me that I'd not seen the system further east, despite there being a number of cultures across the top of Siberia with a very similar way of life.

I'm especially bucked to be able to say I knew someone to whom I could very quickly address such questions, who was able to send me a book on the subject, by return of post (thanks, Carolyn). The reason seems to be that the Communist state collectivised the reindeer of the nomadic Siberian herders. With communal ownership they've had no reason to individually identify stock for several decades, and the practice has become less prevalent. I wander if there are recent changes?

And before we leave the subject of Lapps and reindeer, I can reliably inform you that the quad bike/skidoo and collie dog are second choice. The Lapps have discovered that their herds are so fond of fly agaric toadstools – and their effects – that the whole herd will come trotting if you break some up and scatter it about! And if the little blighters still won't come, I suppose you could pick the pieces up again, and then you soon wouldn't worry about how many reindeer you hadn't gathered. (Oh, all right. **Do not try this at home children!**)

OK, back to sheep. I've pretty much sussed what'll happen, on certain hill farms, when the lunacy of electro-tagging arrives. I don't suppose I should expand on it just here, but I can see the exchange now. 'And whose are all those sheep up there, sir?' 'Dunno, Guvnor. They bin there all summer, but ain't got no tags, only they old ear notches.'

I know it's not a joking matter. The cretinous desk jockeys responsible will remain beyond our reach, while many of us will suffer serious grief because of their thoughtless rules, and total disregard for practicality. Many of us will shed actual ewes, along with 'virtual' ewes, and a tad fewer people will be fed.

Given the opportunity – and as mentioned previously – I'd take these desk jockeys round the back, and peel the little wretches alive. (I'm told that I should recognise that my solutions are widely considered extreme, and I should content myself with a strongly worded letter… Hmm. No, sorry, pass me the sharpening stone.)

Autumn 2008

South Devon cows in the river

As summer turns to autumn the last of harvest will just about be put away, and now the livestock jobs need attention again.

The flocks and herds will soon need to be bought down from the higher pastures. Cows will come down from newtakes and commons onto the in-bye fields to keep some bloom on the calves ready for sale. The ewes will have to be gathered to wean the lambs, so that the ewes can get back in condition before they see the ram later in the autumn. And of course, with pony sales approaching, the mares will have to be 'drifted' off the hill to take off the surplus foals.

It would be a strange livestock farmer who didn't love this time of year. The stock living – as the saying goes – 'off the smell of an oily rag', and the weather still kind, the harvest in the barn. Handling the stock to see how the youngsters have grown on through the summer is a treat.

One of my own favourite tasks is bringing the South Devon cattle home from the newtake where they spend high summer.

Lazy old cows, barging each other along, with calves lost in the press of bodies, bawling for their mother. The bull (Baldric) occasionally grumbling away, just in case anyone forgets he's 'the man'. Flies buzzing around your head, and crawling across the bull's flanks in swarms. He must smell irresistible to the flies. I just like the smell of warm cattle at grass and broken bracken, bellied aside as the girls wend their way down the hill. It is a very special time.

My herd have to cross a couple of rivers to get where they need to be. This means persuading them into fords, which the cows will do soon enough, leaving the calves running up and down the bank. This takes a bit of careful shepherding, but is all part of the fun. The only real problem is if there has been heavy rain upstream, and there is a bit too much water. I have watched recently calved South Devon cows nurse the calves across, keeping them upstream and pressed against their sides by the current.

The Galloway cattle I graze semi-feral further out, on the common, are a different kettle of fish. They bring themselves down to feed later in the year, when floods are a real problem.

41

Galloways on Foxtor

Somehow they know when it's not safe, and just won't cross at all if the water is too high. They'll make the calves swim, if needs be, but only up to a point. Very occasionally the two-year-old heifers might try something rash, and I've had one or two heart-stopping moments watching them swim diagonally through raging torrents, but strangely enough they almost always know what they're doing.

Back to the big orange South Devons. A few years ago we were taking them across the wider crossing they have to negotiate when the young lad helping out noted that the river was up over the stepping-stones, and his trainers were going to get wet. I had reminded him earlier that he'd need his wellies, but he wouldn't hear of it.

As the cows started to amble down the slot worn in the bank, I helpfully suggested that he could always ride a cow across, to save getting wet feet. 'Really?' he asked. 'Oh yes,' I replied, 'Old stockman's trick it is' (and indeed it was). Bless his trusting heart; he selected a mount, and jumped from the bank onto her back. She merely took three steps and sidestepped, dropping him into a foot of water.

Being a responsible employer, and wanting to ensure the lad learned as much as time would allow, I quickly scolded him, telling him he needed to find an older cow that wouldn't be so easily spooked.

So he tried again. The next cow took him a dozen paces into the ford before dumping him into three feet of water, on his back.

Well I enjoyed it anyway.

Nervous ticks

I don't know if it's the season, but the crop of ticks on the dogs has been spectacular. One uncovered on the wife's deerhound (her housedog… ie it's as big as a house), was the size of a blue-grey smartie. When I took it off, it put up quite a struggle. (Mind, finding it on the hound took some doing. Must be like hunting big game in a dense forest!)

That one didn't go on the Aga hotplate – during our lunchtime pastime of 'tick high-jump contests' – as big 'uns smell too much, and don't give as much sport anyway. The best jumpers are generally quite small; the great big munters just sit there and fizz. (You've got to admit the educational value of this book is notable.)

A rather less interesting sport altogether is simply to put some in a marked area and see whose entrant escapes first… (mind the prize for the quickest is to be put on the hotplate first!)

A couple of years ago Alison and I took the kids off to a mixed softwood plantation I had reason to walk carefully; the idea being the small Coakers could run round the trees while I measured and counted, and we could then regroup to have a picnic in some sylvan glade.

Great plan: and it went swimmingly right up until the moment we all settled down in a clearing, relaxing amidst the flickering midsummer sunlight. As we tucked into our grub, I noticed a small tick marching up one of the kid's ankles… then another, and another, and… holy cow! We were being attacked *en masse*. There were dozens and dozens of the little beggars. If you'd have laid down for a snooze, I suspect you'd have awoken with some hundreds of passengers. I suppose we'd happened on the perfect moment for that year's crop, expecting to be alighting on some passing deer.

You've all, no doubt, got your own horror stories about the monsoons this summer, so I don't see much point in going there. I've had no more fun than you, and the quality of what forage we finally made was about what I'd expect. The only nice hay of the year didn't happen until 21 September, which is a bit late, even by my laggardly standards.

Still, better than snowballs, as they say round here.

We have finally got rid of the stupid air suspension on the wife's Discovery. What possessed Land Rover to fit such nonsense is a mystery to me… certainly the designing of a reliable system was beyond them. After years of failed parts and electrics, a coil spring kit was obtained for not much more than the annual compressor replacement bill. Hopefully that's the end of that for a bit. The Disco has otherwise been a useful workhorse; just go for the least-complicated model you can find (I think electronics remain a dark art in Solihull).

Eartags and passports

The autumn round of pre-movement TB testing has included, as well as store cattle and suckled calves, a couple of bulls who're off on working holidays… 'sex tourists' in current phraseology. Anyway, so far so good, and they're champing at the bit.

I am heartily sick of the TB testing regime, passport system and general paperwork. Pity those of you who don't get to play this happy autumnal game, and can only guess the delights of trying to select weeks in advance which youngstock are going where, and getting a test booked for just the moment. Then rodeoing the 'playful' yearlings into the railed-off pens at grass keep to jab them, making sure they've got the appropriate earrings and paperwork, only to get them back in to read the test, hoping that Brock hasn't piddled in the trough. These cattle must be kept under lock and key somewhere handy for loading for the sale but away from the bulls who're also under lockdown, hoping no one tugs out an earring in the meantime etc (am I ranting again?).

It is a fact that any human, reading out loud, or copying down, long lists of complex numbers, will make errors. Drizzle falling on steaming jostling cattle hardly helps matters: the paperwork will be soggy, everything will be plastered in 'reconstituted grass' and, like you, I am only human.

The dark forces of the state, however, make no allowance for such slips, and every error made will be another animal that cannot go to market on the allotted day. I still have to pay the vet, go through all the motions, and then discover that any animal which somehow slipped through the net is left high and dry.

Its gender will have miraculously changed since the day its mother was chasing me round a gorse bush in the rain, trying to lift its tail while defending myself with a pair of tag pliers, or someone somewhere will have transcribed one of the 14 digits wrong. A helpful rambler might have left a gate unlatched on the wrong night, or a store lamb from the previous day's market will have been sent home for developing a sore toe in transit – precipitating a six-day movement standstill. OK. I'll stop there.

And no, I don't have Tourette's syndrome, it really is a %*&$ing nightmare.

On balance, I suppose it's just as well the bullocks aren't worth much. It would break your heart if all the potential slip-ups prevented you from actually coining it!

And on that subject I keep having 25-year flashbacks, when handling a field full of shiny healthy yearling cattle, or a batch of rounded milky chopped suckled calves, thinking to myself what a tidy sum they're going to raise. I easily slip back to when a pen full of cattle was a real paycheque, and something to be relying on. Sadly now they're likely to just about to pay the week's bills.

I was followed through the store ring recently by a colossal big steer (off rather lower ground). The steer topped a thousand, and everyone was suitably impressed. Sadly, as I recall, the same-sized beast would've made pretty much the same sterling price 25 years ago. Sobering.

Yet more socialising – and I'm not out on the razz every night, honest – was recently topped by a marvellously convivial shindig (thrown to celebrate the triumphal return of the host's daughter from the Beijing Olympics, work it out yourself). A munificent spread, and a huge crowd ready to celebrate Heather's fantastic achievement went off as you'd expect. I had a rare old evening, although I'm a bit worried I might've upset one guest, with some more Dad-dancing gags*, and was then caught unawares myself during a spot of my own dance-floor manoeuvres, with a grab in an inappropriate place by another farmer (to be fair, Pete, you've a very gentle touch).

As Alison and I were beating a late retreat a collection of Heather's farming uncles and cousins were fuelled up, arm in arm, and looked like breaking into song.

⋆And I should advise Andrew that I heard Peter Fonda wants that shirt back for the remake of Easy Rider.

Just room enough for one more acerbic observation on humanity.

I'm still finding, when tramping across the veldt looking for stray Scotch ewes, dropped sweetie papers. This perplexes me no end. If you'd gone to all that trouble to hike out into the wilderness, and take in the peaceful serenity of it all, and wonder at the unspoilt beauty, how on Earth can you then drop your trash there? Is it that these people want to embellish the empty moorland landscape with just a homely touch from their urban hole?

I mean, I'm at my place of work, hardly taking in a view I see every day. If I dropped litter I'd be a slovenly arse, and would need remonstrating with. An urban hiker however, who has taken a conscious decision to travel so far for recreation? They must need therapy.

My pal Brian resides in a house beside a fairly popular beauty spot... tumbling brook, medieval granite bridge, lay-by beside gnarled oak trees and huge moss-covered granite boulders, you get the picture.

I've found him, before now, coming out of his front gate of an evening, to pick up the collection of detritus left in the lay-by by the day's visitors. Now Brian is a lucid and far-travelled man, retired from an illustrious career, but is also greatly perplexed by the phenomena. How can they deliberately come to such a place, he speculates, sit and marvel at its beauty, and then walk away from their disposable barbeques, plastic wrappers, empty tins and secondhand nappies?

I strongly suspect that Brian and I have the solution, but it might be seen as a bit too draconian.

Waiter, there's a fly in my soup...

Worried that we might all poke our collective fingers in the machinery, the HSE recently cajoled scores of us to go on a 'Farm Safety and Health Event'. Repeat 'invitations' (thinly veiled threats) persuaded lots of local farms to send someone along. Mostly, the 'Missus' got sent, and it being half-term week this generally meant that the kids then got left with Dad for the day.

That meant they ended up helping tag some fresh autumn calves, or dip the hill ewes. Possibly they could assist around the mill for the day, or shift the bulls⋆ around to keep them away from the heifers… I think I see a flaw in this plan.

⋆*The attendee from these premises came home assuring me that in the far-away fantasy place 'HSE land', all bulls live in custom-made pens, only briefly being allowed out of captivity for a moment's rumpy-pumpy. Ha! In my experience the one thing that's damn sure to make a bull nasty is to lock him away on his own and act as if he is a dangerous wild animal. My advice to you if you have a grumpy bull – if it really is an unsavoury character – is to shoot it. Don't wait til tomorrow, do it today. If however you find you then have another grumpy bull, get out of cattle. The bull isn't the problem.*

Oh, and I was just reading about some heifers on sale somewhere, which were 'Free of the bull, and cycling regularly', which reminded me of a pal of mine who keeps telling me the way forward in cattle is with these here 'stabilisers'. Is there a link?

Instead of a holiday, Alison and I have recently treated ourselves, zipping off for a couple of nights away. We took in some business stuff, and a posh AGM and dinner with a group of individuals who may remain anonymous for reasons that will become apparent.

The journey started poorly, travelling in a wind-up 'Biggles and Algy' aeroplane⋆, flying in a howling gale with torrents of rain. Alison isn't overly enthusiastic about flying at the best of times, and on the last occasion she dug her nails into my palm like that she was about to present me with another child.

⋆*And we note that Exeter aerodrome still has some poorly disguised 'Biggles and Algy' era buildings. I'm pretty sure if you stuck your head in the door shouting 'Scramble chaps' half a dozen moustachioed old buffers in sheepskin flying jackets would creakingly come tumbling out.*

Anyway, we finally got to the posh meal, organised by a group of people who really should have been able to put on a roast beef to beat all others. Strange then that when we asked for the beef we were served with sole. Not Dover or lemon sole, you understand. Boot sole. I think mine might've been synthetic at that. For good measure my roast sole included a dead fly in the gravy for garnish (overleaf).

As she took my empty plate (empty except for the fly that is), I congratulated the waitress on the salubrious insect garnish.

Mmmm... insect garnish

Since the comment went several storeys over her somewhat flat head, that might have been the end of that. But no: when puddings arrived, the nice young lady across the table found a fly in her fruit salad. (A fruit fly, perhaps?) She wasn't quite as hungry as I was, and suggested to the waitress that this wasn't absolutely in order.

Astonishingly (and I can hardly believe this), apart from a pretty insipid apology from Miss Flathead, and a fresh pudding, nothing was said by the kitchen staff or management. What memorable service. Sometimes it's so bad it becomes part of the experience!

Oh well, some very convivial company and the spectacularly wide selection of single malts made for a good night.

I am lucky enough to know a charming couple who you might very well describe as 'smallholders'... I'll omit their location for now. They are lots of fun, and will be the first to admit they don't know much about this farming lark. When they started out, I regularly had to (diplomatically) suggest an alternative work method or stocking regime when one of their hare-brained projects looked like getting out of hand. But being educated and lucid folk they steadily got the hang of things.

Now they have had a house cow on and off, but with a total footprint of about four acres having a bovine about severely restricts their options. I reckon that, with calves born etc, there has been a total of five cattle recorded on the place in the last 30-odd years, all tagged and registered properly. OK? Got the picture?

Right, to cut to the chase. I recently witnessed the following (and I swear I'm not making this up). A visitor arrives at this smallholding, wearing an RPA sweater. She politely announces she's here on a random cattle inspection, as BCMS lists this as premises on which cattle have been kept, and she therefore needs 'To inspect your cattle'. A brief check ensures the official is on the right holding number, and speaking to the occupant. 'Well,' says the occupant, 'we haven't any cattle just now' (and this has indeed been the case for a couple of years). 'Oh we know that,' says the inspector, nice as pie, 'but I still have to come and check anyway.'

Really, really. The nice lady was there to look at cattle she knew not to exist. There was never the least suggestion that she was going to rummage around in the undergrowth to make sure. She was quite happy that she was being told the truth, but orders is orders.

Beware, these people walk among us.

Further education

You'll know by now I admit to being an uneducated peasant hill farmer, so you'll have to understand my thoughts on agri colleges. Whilst I'm happy to see young 'uns taught the science behind farmin' and shown practical management (and I recognise that getting them out from under Mother's skirt is a vital part of their lives) I have long harboured suspicions that finding the trick that gets you through is something you'll never be taught. Whether you learn from what life throws at you, or not, is pretty much the thing, isn't it?

Anyway, I'm greatly tickled by the location and set-up of various surviving agri colleges. One I read about just now boasts it milks 250 cows, lambs 750 ewes at 200 percent, and grows 200–300 acres of cereal. Others sit on rich silt land, in former grand houses.

If any of my hooligans wish to pursue further agri education, I'll be wanting them to attend somewhere that struggles to keep 30 cows, can't stop its 200 ewes from straying, and hasn't got a plough. I don't want it to be called 'Lushly Manor', or 'Deeper Flats'. I'll be looking for a prospectus from 'Bony Crag', or 'Hard-bitten Fell'.

This is, I know, all pretty much pie in the sky. I'll struggle to stop the boy from going straight into work with both feet as soon as he can. I'm thinking of sending him off searching for envelopes of cash left at post office boxes in far-flung countries, just so as he sees some of the world.

And yes, I know I have daughters… Agnes is destined, if she can be bothered – big IF – to be a killer barrister. She absorbs the written word like a sponge, and will forcibly argue any point, on general principles, forever. Polly meanwhile seeks only to be a ballerina (or possibly a princess).

I'm running a book on these matters if any of you fancies a wager!

I did once attend some hill-farming seminar, greatly impressing some lady delegates with my incisive comments on the topic under discussion, then offending them to the point of being an utter bounder. My crime being that I voiced that I'd rather like the idea of my son being able to stand in my boots on my demise. 'But what of your daughters, Mr Coaker?' 'They're daughters,' I responded, going on to suggest that as I've only the one pair of boots, better they get used to the idea of looking for their own path in life. I was immediately downgraded to caveman status.

Now since I know that it isn't just peasants wot read this drivel, I want to take this opportunity to offer a stern warning to those readers without dirt under their nails... The munificent cereal harvest in both the Eastern European plain and North American prairies have absolutely not resolved the global food shortage. The underlying factors have not gone away, and it would have only taken a brief drought, early in the season, in either of those breadbaskets, to have had the most profound effect on the matter.

I suppose reasonably bright urban people in positions of influence can see the implications, but I struggle to see what they do about it (seemingly Mr Benn thinks we had 'a record harvest' in the UK in 2008. Why yes we did old chap, if you want to eat cattle feed).

Meanwhile, some of these urban persons are still frantically trying to prop up the housing market, and therefore, they think, the rest of the known world.

I rarely venture into the subject on the grounds that I am eminently unqualified to do so. But I've got a couple of pointy thoughts on the subject.

Propping up anything over-inflated won't make it any more viable until the ground shifts beneath your feet. And the shift isn't always then in the direction you might expect. The fact remains that too many people have borrowed too much on, and against, garbage. Too many people want to live above their means, doing jobs that are, in all honesty, superfluous.

I rather suspect that being told we have to face up to a period of painful austerity is something we might not want to hear.

And just recently (sorry if the world has turned since time of writing), it occurs to me that lowering interest rates to stimulate more lending by banks which are cash-strapped will also pressure that cash reserve. If those lending to the bank get nothing in return, won't they just look for somewhere else to put that money? What happens if they start to move it out of the mainstream UK economy? I don't know how taking currency out of a country works, but I'll bet you a quid (on this as well) that it is a subject that will be in some minds.

Look, I'm too simple to get a handle on all this. I'll just go on feeding cattle.

Wooden sheep

Ah, now I hadn't seen my pal Reece for a while. He sporadically appears to buy improbably large chunks of wood, to hew even more improbable sculptures. He turned up again t'other day, seeking more trunks to turn into wooden sheep. (These have several attractive advantages over actual sheep, as I understand things. They eat nothing, rarely stray, never go lame, have no eartags, and sell for rather more than ordinary sheep. Woodworm might become an issue, but you can't have it all.)

Anyway, it was a pleasure to see Reece again, him being quite a character. He's had a varied career, having been apprenticed to a taxidermist in his youth, and then done a bit of turkey inseminating, prior to taking up sculpture professionally.★ He admits these previous jobs are – should he start to discuss them in any great detail at the bar – pretty sure to get him chucked out of the pub. I would deferentially suggest, Reece, that perhaps less graphic descriptions would allow you to finish your pint!

Having noted his absence, I politely enquired what he'd been up to? 'Not much, on account of having a fractured skull,' Reece explained. 'Oh,' I exclaimed, quite concerned, 'how did you come to do that?'

'Extreme gardening,' came the reply.

★*I know one or two sculptors, and I note that several of them have more than a passing interest in anatomy. One, who sculpts in clay to subsequently cast stunning bronzes, sometimes starts out by sketching the most fantastic pencil drawings of his subject's skeletal workings. I would have thought his drawing was every bit as good as his sculpting.*

Fascinating!

One of Reece's sheep *www.reeceingram.co.uk*

On the subject of knife possession amongst the rural unwashed... A few of us were recently asked to go to the House of Lords to make polite comment to a number of ministers of state, top DEFRA doofers and a selection of the great and the good. It was only good fortune that some of the girls remembered to make damn sure we'd emptied our pockets of the sharpened instruments of our trade first! The security geezers mightn't have approved!

It was the kind of place where 'one' collects one's name badge on arrival, so everyone knows who one is. Those labels prepped for the peasants invited merely referred to 'Fred Bloggs – Farmer, Dartmoor', whereas greater personages had their titles printed in full: 'The Earl This', or 'Lord That'. I notice those types listed no gainful employment – maybe just being a nob is a job in itself.

Well I got up to the table where the badges wuz all rowed up, and could I find mine… no chance (I wasn't gate crashing this time, honest). After a fruitless search I decided I'd simply half inch someone else's. I rather fancied being an Earl for the day, or at the very least a 'Sir'. Conversation with one of the penguins on duty revealed that 'The Countess of Blobbyland' was likely to be a no-show, but we agreed that I'd never pull it off. I had neither the cleavage nor the moustache.

I should add that my habitual enquiries revealed that the penguins and sweet things in skirts handing round the drinkie-poos and canapés came from a variety of countries, across the Med, and through Eastern Europe. None was English. Oh, and the volume of booze put in front of the nobs was scary. The moment your glass was half empty a dapper little bloke was at yer elbow to top you up. I kept to orange juice for fear of making a bigger arse of myself than usual!

I note I was the only male attendee not wearing a collar and tie, being adorned in my cultural attire of checked lumberjack shirt, harvester strides, and heavy leather boots (my only footwear). I see no problem with this, although Alison despairs. As it happens, the first thing delegates met, on entering the room, was a copy of the photo of dun Belt bull Conq and I – as per front cover – blown up and covering half the wall.

I did take the opportunity of ear-bending a very top snivel servant (Layland grabbed his arm, while I stood on his foot), but wise hands steered the ministers present well away from my grasping reach. (The new boy seems to be both a failed farmer and a party apparatchik.)

Anyway, onwards to other matters of state.

I have to admit that I haven't been selected as a suitable candidate for the much discussed 'Council of Food Policy Advisors' despite, or possibly because of, a carefully worded letter requesting a voice at that particular table. Looking at the list of seats initially filled, Sir Don Curry seems to be the only one who'd actually know how food is grown.

Ho-hum. Good luck folks. Do try to remember the phrase 'bread riots' before we have the chance to witness them first hand. (Secretly, I only really applied cos I wanted to be ordered about by the chairperson, one 'Dame Suzi Leather'.)

I'm not going to bore you with much news here. It's summed up with the sawmill being dead quiet, on account of the builders all having gone to ground, and my farming career enjoying troughs equal to, or greater than, the peaks.

Some of the troughs have been pretty wretched, while the peaks have been just high enough to catch some sun and keep me going through the winter.

And lastly, I should remind some of you that, despite your protestations, sending me an email via your 'Blackberry' does not count as one of your 'five fruit and veg a day'.

Gordon's in trouble

I feel no embarrassment about my Olympiad standard of tightfistedness. In fact, I wear it as a badge of honour. So you'll be pleased to hear my log sales have been very buoyant recently (about the only bit of the timber job that is), and supplies are being eked out with logs hewn from a monstrous stand of gorse.

A couple of us have recently been spending an hour or two in amongst this thicket with first the loader tractor⋆, then the chainsaw, then the tractor again, and lastly a pot of Round Up. Careful analysis showed that the time spent filling a dumpy bag with cut gorse logs was pretty well spent. (The only hang-up being consumer resistance to these logs, which can warm your hands at every stage of the consumption. Bargain I'd have thought!)

Technique. Drive into thicket with loader and twin spikes flat on floor. When traction becomes an issue, lift loader, ripping out half of what hasn't already snapped off. Take resulting pile of material to bonfire, remember not to place tractor above flickery orange bits (while praying fervently that tractor doesn't fail near flickery orange bits).

The results vary, but the crucial bit remains not to try and reverse out of a real heavy area lest you disembowel the tractor on the swept-over tank traps (**you are not advised to try this at home, boys and girls**).

Anyone wishing to show me how this is so much easier with a flail/swipe/mulcher of some kind is very welcome to have a go. I'll draw you a map of the boulders just as soon as you've finished!

The more astute will have noticed that the pot of Round Up is probably the most important part of the operation, and I suspect you're right. The next step is to hem some sheep in on it, and let their nibbling little ways rip out next spring's seedlings, which will come up pretty much like a carpet.

The boy has been helping me on this project after school time, feeding a fire or using a handsaw in amongst the jungle.

Given that his beddy-bye stories as a toddler were read from a 1965 Galloway cattle journal, and that he had to help lamb his own Scotch ewes pretty soon after that, the poor little blighter never stood a chance, did he?

I've been giving this some thought, recalling that my Dad and I spent a day or two every spring, with a box of matches each, in amongst the above-mentioned gorse. I'm too embarrassed to mention that the 1965 Galloway journal has been kicking around ever since, but recognise the ongoing issues these parenting techniques raise.

Speaking of Galloways, is there a change in the breeze? I notice that pretty much all of my spare hairy little heifers are now spoken for, some months in advance. Not just the odd surplus pedigree Belted or Riggit you understand, but the mis-marks and cross-breds as well. Meanwhile, without realising it, I notice suddenly the Galloway bulls keep on going out on hire. The South Devon and Angus bulls I'd expect to have the odd jaunt out and about, but Conqueror, the dun Belt, is hardly ever home at the minute. I hope he's having fun. Beggar doesn't send me any postcards.

To load the old grumbler I just open the ramp of the trailer in the middle of the yard. He pretty much leaps up, knowing what such a journey might mean! (Well, wouldn't you?)

Those of you who make cracks about Galloways' behavioural issues should meet him. I've had some ridiculously quiet South Devon bulls over the years, but Conq takes the biscuit. OK, so he grumbles almost constantly, but it's just talk. (The noise is halfway between a bass whale song and some half-heard underground rumbling, resonating just at the bottom of human audible range. Following him along a hard track, you feel the noise through your feet.) But get in close with him and he's like an old house cow. Happily, most of his progeny are inheriting his dopey nature.

And speaking of dopey, you'll recall Alison has an elegant but idle deerhound called Millie, who spends most of her time lying

Millie

in front of the Aga, fasto (Millie, not Alison that is). This seems to be a deerhound's natural habitat.

Sawyer Barry reckons she's evolving into a hearthrug. Pretty soon, he assures us, her eyes will migrate to one side of her head, like a baby flatfish. (You had forgotten that, hadn't you? Flounders and dabs and the like are hatched like any other fish, swimming along upright, with an eye on each side. Then they suddenly tip over, and one eye migrates!)

To move us onto rather wider topics, can I ask… isn't the world expecting rather too much of Obama just now?

Poor young pup. He's walked – 'on water' apparently – into a monstrous recession, and has no magic wand to wave.

And back here, Gordon is still trying to pump money into banks, which – as my simple farmer's understanding has it – have been lending more than they should, against highly dubious assets. I can well understand that the banks will want to rein in lending for several reasons, and am nonplussed that Gordon is so determined that they should keep lending more. Wasn't he always the one for dour-faced warnings to be prudent?

I don't suppose he's remembered the commodity price spark that helped ignite things in the first place. Perhaps he thinks it's gone away.

Oh, and while we're in politics land, we all know that wanting to be an MP should absolutely be a disqualifying characteristic for a candidate, but the furore over Labour Lords using their sway for a few thousand quid suggests that there are some pretty fundamental questions that need asking about the ways members of either house earn a crust. I suspect by the time you lot read this these questions will be more prominent.

'It's snowing outside boys and girls.'
'Oh no it isn't!'

We had a night out recently, taking the kids and Grandma to the Postbridge village panto. In the tradition of small community pantos, the players are mostly known well (if not actually related) to the audience, and therefore vice versa. This ensures there is usually a fair bit of heckling going either way, and this year was no exception. (Mind, when the prompt lost his place, the ad-libbing reached hitherto unseen levels. A vintage performance.)

At the halftime interval though, a new element surfaced. One or two souls realised that the flurries of snow we'd driven through to get there had turned into a full-on blizzard, and half the audience got up and decamped. The cast rattled through the rest of the panto to a half-empty hall, and we finally stumbled out into a whiteout, with the roads already inches deep. More snow fell like it would never stop.

Hmm, said I. We hurriedly said our goodbyes, loaded up the Disco, and went to leave. As I got in, one of the cast – 'Baron Hardup', who was bound for Ashburton – asked if I'd be good enough to follow him as far as Dartmeet, to see that he got up the other side. 'Okey dokey,' I rashly volunteered, and off we went.

Along the level, from Postbridge back towards Princetown, things went along well enough. A lifetime of careering across slippy slidy hillsides teaches proficiency in no sudden turns or braking. Visibility was an issue as the world was reduced to a 50-yard circle, and driving into heavy snow is extremely odd. After a while the disorienting way the snow flakes come flying out of the dark at the windscreen becomes hypnotic, and far more interesting than such mundane matters as watching where the road goes, or making sure the good Baron was still up front. (I was already wandering how I was going to flag him down and stop him trying the descent down into Dartmeet. He was never gonna make it back up, and I really didn't want to venture down the steep to rescue him.)

Still, on we went until we got to Two Bridges Cross, where we should all have turned left. But no, the Baron went straight on – oh yes he did! 'Bless me,' I said, wandering if I'd been following the wrong car all the way, and did that mean his Baronship was now stuck in a drift, somewhere unnoticed, on my watch… gulp.

We followed the car down to Two Bridges, where it slewed gracefully to a halt at the bottom of the slope. Happily it was the Baron, aka Jonny. He assured me that he and the steering wheel had turned left, but the rest of the car disagreed, and sailed straight on. I suggested it might be time to abandon 2WD, and he could have lodgings for the night. He concurred. With the good Baron aboard, we set off once more.

Out across Dunnabridge Common the road had disappeared completely, and I was navigating by the road signs and trying to recall the topography. With the back of the wagon filled with my family and a guest, Alison and I quietly discussed which direction I was going to have to walk in to locate a tractor to recover us… but somehow we made it back home.

The Baron and I had to have a pretty serious snort, and the kids won't forget that trip to the panto for a while.

The following morning bought a certain amount of 'local difficulty'. The council sent out a snowplough, which in turn had to be recovered by several tractors. The spindrift was blowing off the tops of Down Ridge and Terhill like they were on fire, and looking out across the line of tors behind Powdermills the whole skyline was lost in a haze of the drifting stuff.

Alison took the boy out to find his 32-year-old mare, and after they'd been gone half an hour I did start to worry. (They all turned up, the mare having found a sensible place to get out of the wind.)

By lunchtime the drifts were over the tops of the walls, and I was wading waist-deep, digging out gates, to get things fed. Strangely none of the lads got in, and it was a long day for an old bloke.

I suppose we should be profoundly grateful that it was into February, not early in January. The drifts are mostly gone two weeks later, although I'm hearing some are still yielding dead ewes. (I dug for one in a small group of skinnies I'm feeding near the yard. Stupid creature was buried again the next day, and is no longer with me. The Scotties on the hill have mostly turned up fine.)

Ho-hum. Still, my Dad and his generation farmed through '63 and '47, each of which killed serious amounts of stock. Half the sheep in many cases. Think on that.

Ten feet of rain at my end of the pool

As I may have mentioned, I'm no big lover of grey squirrels. This state was greatly reinforced t'other day when we ventured into a mixed wood I planted about 15 years ago. Thinking we'd fill in some gaps before the sap started rising, we set off with a bag of plants and a spade each. I've had to fill in holes before after a tribe of fallow deer started squatting thereabouts, and have had various bunny troubles to boot, and fight occasional battles with some gorse at the top of the bank… still there's a goodly number of trees showing some height now. Along the sheltered lower run a fine crop of oak brings pleasure to the eye. Already topping 20 feet, and as thick as your thigh, with a bit of formative pruning leaving many straight and single. Just as it should be. Until that is, squirrels took a fancy to 'em. Little swines.

They've ring-barked every other one at about 8 feet. This doesn't kill the tree straight off, just allows the top to snap out, rot to come in, and the subsequent growth to resemble oversize mops rather than the ships' masts of my desire. For good measure they uncannily pick the trees with the best form, ignoring (or is it ig-gnawing?) those that have bent sideways to look for light, or that've forked beyond redemption.

The only recourse is to coppice each tree to ground level, and let it fight its way up through the bunnies, gorse and Bambis all over again. I can't say I'm especially pleased about this state of affairs, and have left some little blue snacks for the vermin, stuffed in tubes up in the air.

I've found growing a crop of trees deeply therapeutic, and don't really care that it costs more than it will ever earn. Perhaps my progeny will be in a position to harvest something which will pay for future replanting. Given that my sawmilling business relies on the forethought of others, I'm inclined to do a bit in return.

Anyway, run down, shoot or poison every one of the little grey arboreal rats you see. Too many still won't be enough.

The snow and general wintry weather has been causing me a certain amount of bother, but I expect you can tell your own tales about that. Just one brief factoid for you, then. I may have alluded to the high rainfall hereabouts, and the fact that it seems to have dragged the stock after two wet summers. Well, a rain gauge on a hill 2½ miles south of here, upon the northern slopes of which my Galloways roam, recorded 124 inches last year. That's just over 10 feet, or 3 metres if you'd rather. And you wonder why I comment on it occasionally?

Speaking of the livestock, I've had a run of it this week.

Sunday saw a 10-year-old Galloway – in a shed full of dry cows – off her legs. Why? I've no idea. Perhaps the South Devon bull knocked her over, or she had somehow got cast behind a pretty minor ridge in the poop. Couldn't say. She was bright, and ate and drank freely, and what went in went through OK. To save her being trampled by her chums, Alison and I got her pulled out into the hay shed next door. Nothing too severe, and she moved easily enough. She was still bright and happy, got to her feet briefly even. Then, come Monday morning… was dead as dog's doings.

Monday also found the quietest of the weaned Dartmoor foals uncomfortable with colic. We separated him out, but didn't tell the kids, who'd been haltering him. And now have to tell 'em he was a goner by Tuesday morning.

Tuesday afternoon – today – bought news that one of the Belts down in the valley is toes up beside the river. Young Joe went down to check, and reports it is the one that's been mooching about and hanging back. Nothing clearly wrong, just hanging back. I'm suspicious of waste plastic blockage. However careful you are, a bit of string or net can sneak through can't it? I'm told they build up into a ball.

Now we have the delightful task of trying to extricate her. I have had a tractor within a few hundred feet of her location, but only in very dry weather, and not for some decades. Luckily I've been down there with a box of matches a couple of weeks ago, so we can at least see some of the boulders.

Hey-ho. I've reminded poor Joe that the numbers are about to start going upwards again, as lambs and calves start.

First however, we have to hurdle the next obstacle. The annual trial by TB test is almost upon us, and I'm some worried. I've got Galloway youngstock promised to three Dartmoor folk, two Cornish, and a Yorkshire man, and there's various bulls due to go out sold or on hire to two different Dartmoor men, another Cornishman, and a Galloway bull calf due to travel to Scotland. On top of that I ought to shift a few steers in the spring store sales.

I did toy with doing a few batches beforehand, in case of trouble, but where would I start?

Suppose I'll just let the dice roll as things stand. I haven't had any problems to date, but who the hell knows now, eh?

Oh well. Gotta get on and see how much rope I can rustle up.

Spring 2009

Breakfast nailed

The back end of winter has been pretty tiresome, trying to persuade the old girls to eat the remaining sludge baled in last year's monsoons. I kept back some of the best stuff for the yearlings and such, but that wasn't going to go far enough.

It would be fair to say that several of my cattle have caught the short end of the stick in this respect.

Two different lots have been reluctantly eating the soggy output made Widecombe Fair week, and another group have been on round-bale hay made some months after its sell-by date. Most of these cattle came through the winter looking like they'd rather belong to someone else.

I think a colleague and I hit the nail on the head when we realised it wasn't hard winters that were dragging us and the stock; it was not having a summer in between that was the root of the problem.

Meanwhile, spring has sprung around the yard, and the feral bantams are fussing about all over the place. Never having enough eggs, the boy persuaded his mother to take him to buy half a dozen 'proper' point-of-lay hybrids, which he housed in a stone outbuilding. He followed the instructions given to the letter, giving them extended daylight with a lamp on a timer.

And now? There are six eggs a day coming out of them, and all the bantams are laying for Queen and Country too. Can't eat all the blinking things. The boy gives any visitors the hard sell to see if he can shift another box, and Alison has had to take up baking in a big way.

Speaking of the boy, I've got to tell you of yet another indication of how mean I am. When he was a toddler, he shovelled his porridge with a plastic-handled spoon he'd found somewhere. This handle soon broke, and he was left gripping his favourite spoon by the short tang remaining – he's a determined little blighter, I'll give him that. Anyway, we agreed that would never do, so Daddy fixed it up just fine with the welder and a 6-inch nail… hey presto! (Years later his mother might have her head in her hands, but it's still his favourite.)

John's spoon

Sorry, back to spring. Now I speculated backalong on whether the cuckoos' victims know what awaits them when they hear the parasites call.

Well I've been looking into this, and indeed they do. There is a long-standing and complex warfare going on between various host birds and the different types of cuckoo, far more involved than I'd assumed.

Various cuckoo populations have evolved eggshell patterns to match their specific target species, so they don't get hooked straight out of the nest. These variations are passed along female cuckoo lines, with males siring chicks irrespective. Then, as you already know, the first thing a cuckoo chick does, on hatching, is chuck any remaining eggs/hatchlings out of the nest.

Something that puzzles me, though, is how does the cuckoo chick know what it is?

If a 'lesser-crested puddle hopper' rears a cuckoo, wouldn't the chick think it's a 'lesser-crested puddle hopper'? No, it knows it is a cuckoo, and, if it is a lady cuckoo, it then just targets the host species that reared it. Wow, double wow!

Elsewhere it gets even stranger. A European cuckoo species is understood to practise a Mafia-type extortion policy. If the hosts – magpies in this case – reject a cuckoo's egg, the latter spends all spring making damn sure the magpie doesn't rear any chicks of her own either. Compliant magpie populations get to rear their own chicks occasionally, and there is evidence that they're evolving docility in this respect.

This is all too much for my head.

Imagine a species our size, and smarter than us doing that – oh yes, John Wyndham did, didn't he?

Invisible peasants

Hey, some bloke researching a telly programme has been in touch. He's looking for folk who're still doing work as their forefathers might've done. He understood that somewhere in the backwoods there are still peasants doing those rural tasks just like those shown on old prints from ages past. I believe he envisaged men drystone walling, shepherds fettling sheep's feet, farmers' wives churning butter perhaps. You know the kind of thing. His enquiries had led him to Dartmoor, and thence to you know who.

And how was he communicating about these rare pockets of bucolic living history? Why, by email of course.

I have to say that his lines of enquiry on the subject came within a hair's breadth of being extremely condescending, although he just about got away with it.

Then, when he got to visit, and wander up through the in-bye with me, we walked through a herd of South Devons whose presence on the farm predates the Breed Society, the motor car and most of the modern world by some decades. Brother-in-law Frank was at the top of the field, plonking lumps of granite onto a drystone wall (albeit with a JCB). I don't think he really grasped it at all.

I even shared with him a piece of local rhyming doggerel that suggests that my own peasant tribe and a couple of others were hereabouts when 'The Conqueror came'. Sadly it went over his head. We left the cows grazing where they'd been for a century and a half, and Frank superannuating a wall originally piled up in the Bronze Age, and I let him go on his way.

Meanwhile, some foreign filmmaker type – and I'm not allowed to say he's French, 'cos he's from Corsica – has discovered our pal Colin, in West Cornwall. For several months now, Alban – who is a really nice kid as it goes – has followed Colin about his Bronze Age fields, filming him as he carries out a range of rural tasks (almost) unchanged since time immemorial. Alban suggests Colin is '*magnifique,* 'ee is zee, 'ow you zay? An aboriginal!'

Happily some of Colin's non-stop banter has also gone over Alban's head. This is a film you will want to see, although one assumes it'll firmly have to be aired after the watershed.

And on the subject of non-PC humour, what's this I've been reading about the wailing and gnashing of teeth within rugby officialdom? It appears a local club has had to be severely censured for allowing some off-colour jokes to circulate. Eh? Rugger buggers prevented from relaying off-colour jokes?

Clearly the world around me is a rather different place to how you and I had previously come to regard it, and is possibly rather the poorer for the change.

I don't know if any of you have noticed, but DEFRA have taken to turning up at some bigger store cattle marts and sheep fairs with their travelling road show. The rationale is, I'm told, that it will give them the chance to explain various – and very sensible and well thought out – schemes and rules. (You know, EID for sheep, cost sharing for diseases and the like.)

The nice DEFRA staff turn up in their corporate logo shirts, all freshly scrubbed and eager to help us understand their new world order. And what do we do? Rather disappointingly, we concentrate on getting our beasts penned, and the paperwork completed. We'll be wanting to see who has brought in the best-looking tups, or which bunch of steers takes our eye.

There's the trailer to get washed out, before we head for the tea shack to share in the ritual rounds of cuppas and bacon butties. Old pals to chat to – sometimes not seen from one fair to the next – fat to chew and sticks to lean on. As the auctioneer calls us to attention, and we gather round the sale ring, spare a thought for the poor berks manning the road show… all alone, with no one to talk to except the mineral rep who no one's talking to either.

And speaking of 'the rules', spring has seen me dutifully trying to tag the new calves. This is a bit of an adrenaline rush out on the veldt. When you grab a fresh Galloway, and it bawls, Mother and a couple of Aunties will quickly come bellowing over, and circle you eyeball to eyeball, like the old Redskins going round the covered wagons.

I've found the trick is – having picked your moment carefully – to tip the calf up, drop the ring pliers and tagging gear straightaway, and be ready with the long-handled crook. A few daps on the nose of each circling cow releases a few endorphins, and calms 'em down a bit. Quickly drop the crook, grab the pliers etc, do what needs doing, and 'retire immediately'. (Who needs theme-park rides or extreme sports?)

So far I've been lucky in my choice of the whens and wheres, but our thoughts are with a local colleague (and his family) who had cause to handle a new calf rather sooner than its Mother thought appropriate, and wasn't so lucky. Last I heard he was still in intensive care.

It is in light of the above that you can understand why some of us regard DEFRA's anal fixation with ear tags and paperwork as somewhat out of touch with reality.

I treat the 'cast-iron rules' as more of a rough set of guidelines. A wish list if you will. (I believe I am in a not-very-exclusive group.)

Ghurkas, expenses and swine flu

In case I want to move on from my current employment, I've been scanning the job ads again. One catches my eye. The Met Office have been looking for a (and I'm quoting here) 'Trainee Weather Observer'. Hmm, is that someone whose job it is to look thoughtfully up at the sky, and advise that he thinks, 'Hmm. Looks like rain'?

With some guidance, and diligent study, this trainee might eventually be able to say 'You know, it really does look like rain.' Obviously, it would be several long years of graft and guidance before he'd be allowed to tell us 'It is raining.'

Sadly, reading further down the ad, I see I am manifestly unqualified to observe the weather, even as a trainee.

I'll just have to go on standing in it without observing it.

OK. There's some topical stuff I don't quite get.

In my very limited understanding of such things, catching swine flu now – whilst it is new to our immune system but not so virulent that it's going to kill too many of us – is probably better than catching it in a year's time, when it might very well have mutated into something that will kill piles of us! Given the government's response so far, I presume they discretely concur. ('Cover up your mouth when you cough'? Shades of Hancock.)

Next. If MPs were/are legally allowed to claim for the expenses they have, why bleat about it? Make changing the system an issue for re-election if you will, and hammer any of them who've broken such slack rules, but do move on.

Lastly – and most sensitively I suppose – the Ghurkhas. If they were not promised residency here on signing up, why the angst now? They took well-paid jobs as mercenaries, expecting to return home comparatively wealthy men. I have no issue with any of this. Why back-pedal now?

For the record, I'm sure they are all capital fellows, and will make model citizens here – honestly, I know no ill of them whatsoever – but isn't the UK getting, well, a bit full?

One of my ex-MOD advisers tells me I'm out of touch, and I realise I might only be mentioning the subject in the vague hope that Ms Lumley will come round and give me a thorough telling off. I'd be prepared, in this eventuality, to admit I'd been a very naughty boy.

🦋

I don't recall just why I was reminded of wedding lists recently, but that led me to reminisce about one such list, long ago, from a couple both near and dear.

I was shortly to depart on a grand tour of the Antipodes, and several of us had repaired to a hostelry to share a convivial libation celebrating my pending journey. As the evening wore on, conversation turned to the family wedding I was going to miss (for 'twas my sister Sue and her beau Frank who were to wed). Although the wedding was some months distant, the bride-to-be had already started to consider her wedding list, which was duly circulated for our perusal. We thought the contents of the list very restrained, modest even. Being helpful souls, we grabbed a biro and, when Sue's back was turned, helpfully added some additional small items the couple would find useful.

I'm not sure who put their name down for the new tractor, or the 20 acres of 'off ground' on which to rear the heifers, but I recall that I drew the 'fresh Suffolk ram'.

🦋

Meanwhile, a local kid has almost been chucked off the primary school bus recently. Some geek remeasured the distance from home, and found it 100 yards short of the 2-mile limit (although the bus route goes past his folks' farm entrance). Obviously, he could walk to school couldn't he?

To walk this route the poor little tyke would have to trudge over a pass that crosses a 1210-foot hilltop ridge. It is also a matter of fact that his failure to do this through winter blizzards would count as truancy. I wish I could tell you I'm making this up, but I can't. Happily, the education authority hadn't taken into account his Mum's… er… 'decisive' manner.

I'm also in trouble over another skool matter – big skool this time. I am one of those nasty parents who objects to their kids having to use a computer, outside skool, to complete their homework. Failure to provide kids with a PC and Internet access at home apparently places them on the back foot.

They can, I'm pointedly told, do this homework on a skool computer, during break time. Oh! So kids without this techno back-up at home have to forfeit their playground social-interaction time? (Arguably the most important bit of the educational process.)

I am very uncomfortable with this. Of course our kids do get use of the PC when they need it (and can certainly run rings round me on it), but that's hardly the point.

Anyway, don't panic. My hoodlums are given extra-curricular lessons in the real deal. They can, after a fashion, weld two bits of steel together, hammer nails and vaguely control the dogs. They can lamb a ewe, push cattle along a track, grow all manner of vegs, stitch shirts, and generally remember which words not to use in front of Granny.

Junior driving lessons

SUMMER 2009

Speaking (and exposure) in public

For reasons I can't really explain, the sawmill is absolutely full bore.

To try and keep various teams of oak framers busy Barry and I are, by turn, running the main breakdown saw seven days a week. Chris, our main round timber haulier, is fetching in two lorry loads a week, and my little flatbed is wearing a groove out through the gate delivering sawn goods. Organising the supply of oak logs a month ahead of when we need them is another headache.

Happily the frantic rush coincided with the cattle being turned away, lambing petering out, and the mowing ground having been just stood up. (What happens if we're still under pressure when the grass needs cutting is another matter, and coming up fast.)

Everything ground to a halt anyway this afternoon when the main mill chewed up some important bits in its innards. (This means the 'breakdown saw' is now 'broken down'.) For good measure, the big tractor that lives tied to the timber crane has come out in sympathy, and developed severe incontinence.

I do enjoy the intensity of the pressure, but recognise that if I let it worry me I'd be a goner in a fortnight!

To better myself, I've been trying to read book of quotations (Winston Churchill being one of the best sources, and who recommended just such studies).

The theory is that I'll benefit from other, wiser, folk's wit and wisdom. Problem is of course that I can never remember this wisdom, and next I'll have to obtain a book on improving my memory.

(I'm vaguely aware that there are all sorts of such 'self-help' books. 'Improve your memory', 'How to win friends and influence people', etc, but then recall the twits I've met over the years who've bought them. They're absolutely positive that reading such gibberish will turn their lives around, whereas the truth is, of course, that they're really only enriching some author.)

Perhaps I'll make fame and fortune collating a book of reasons why you shouldn't bother with such stuff.

Poor Alison has been rushing about trying to register the Dartmoor foals before some deadline. Those born after this deadline will have to be microchipped by the vet at a cost rather greater than the value of a colt foal. (Can you guess what will happen to the surplus colts, boys and girls?)

Onwards. Ahh! I've accepted a couple of speaking engagements again. I had tried to give them up, saying I wanted to spend more evenings with the family (please don't hold a grudge if I've turned down your flower-arranging club). This excuse was quite true, but it was also really because I seemed unable to speak at any function – and I mean any function – without wearing the trousers with the bust zip. (You have been warned, Margaret). I'm sure a psychiatrist would point to some unresolved issues.

Anyroad, one local group has promised a free feed, and seeing as I usually pay to attend that particular function anyway, I accepted like a shot. The other group, further away, have promised me hard coin, plus diesel money, and all the beer I can drink over the weekend event. Ha! They're in for a surprise aren't they?

And for the record, the diary is now shut again, and will only reopen for stupid amounts of cash, and I will be almost certainly be wearing the bust trousers!

Lastly, the torrential summer downpours t'other day reminded me of a group of sixth-form students we had camping down in the valley, one long-ago summer. They were washed out by a dreadful wet August week, and were soon packing up to retreat. Bedraggled youths were strewn everywhere. Some lugged gear back to the minibus, while others appeared in the yard, wanting to phone Mum to say they were on the way home – this being before mobile phones. I found one girl out by the back door, shivering cold and sorting her wringing wet gear. Being a kindly man, I suggested she ought to warm herself by the Aga before setting off again. Bless her heart, she timidly crept into the kitchen, and gratefully leant her shivering, goose-pimpled, and… um… lithe bones against the stove…. in just her sodden T-shirt and scanties.

As it happened, the lads were in having a sandwich, having been rained off any harvest work. For some reason, her arrival caused the lunchtime banter to falter, as sandwiches stopped halfway from bait box to mouth. I think a couple of 'em stopped breathing as well, 'til she'd warmed up enough to go on her way again.

Still, helped the lads pass another day.

Jackdaws in the dovecote

Isn't it nice that Hilary Benn has been out on the world stage, pushing for increased production of food?

Sadly, his worthy rhetoric belies his views at home. HB certainly doesn't seem to notice how policy he helps steer is reducing production at a pretty alarming rate. Quite apart from the poor economics of the job, in several parishes locally cattle numbers are struggling to keep up with the TB culling, and sheep numbers on the high ground* are already declining.

*Land occupied by hill farmers isn't by definition the 'moral high ground'. That is just a coincidence.

🦋

Hey, our friend Harriet is thinking about going to uni to study astrophysics. (Ha, it's not exactly rocket science… Oh, it is, isn't it?)

🦋

Wildlife goings-on include the noisiest hatch of jackdaws in Christendom, reared in one of the old dovecotes let into the wall of the longhouse. Whenever mother jackdaw appeared with some grub, the cacophony has been astonishing. We love it. There's also clutches of wrens and (pied?) wagtails and redstarts and blackbirds and robins reared or still rearing all around the yard. (How the poor blighters in the sawmill building cope when the machinery is running I couldn't tell you.)

There's not so many swallows here this year, and no house martins at all, but we have seen and heard any number of cuckoos.

And gathering for shearing, Alison and I clocked five herons on a 200-yard stretch of the West Dart.

🦋

Meanwhile, back during lambing and calving I saw two events I've never witnessed before.

First a Riggit heifer calved, all OK with the calf up and sucked. Before I passed that way again she'd wandered over to a Scotch ewe, freshly lambed nearby, and adopted the single

Scotch lamb. Honestly. She absolutely doted on it, and was pretty unconcerned about her 'bigger' baby. The poor ewe was in a right 'two and eight', as she was constantly being pushed away from the lamb, which was being licked into the ground by his 'big' Mum.

I drove them apart, thinking they'd sort it all out. Not a bit of it. Next morning the heifer was following the lamb about, calf forgotten. In the end I had to move her elsewhere.

Then – and I promise you this is the truth – a Belt heifer calved down amongst the riding ponies, and blowed if one of them didn't nick the calf! This is a mare that's never bred, but was furiously cleaning the calf for all she was worth, whilst the heifer stood back… confused.

That one at least was easily sorted out. Still, twice in a season!

Right, I'm off to persuade the last few Galloways back in the gate, to see their husband.

Bad-tempered peasants

There are a couple of nuggets of farmy news that have been widdling me off of late, and which need exposing to the greater world.

Mapping. For their own special reasons – and by that I mean 'for no reason a sane man would contemplate' – DEFRA are once again mapping the entire English landscape. They have done this several times already, yet surprisingly, with the possible exception of bits of ground lost to the sea, or concrete, they'll find the land area hasn't changed much.

We have barely finished 'discussing' the changes uncovered during the last of these futile exercises and the implications they have on the various enviro-schemes I'm signed into – someone somewhere is greatly excited about whether a dirt track crossing a 250-acre newtake is a 'field' or a 'road', someone else is fretting whether the scrap of garden beside a long-derelict miner's cottage is 'improved pasture' or not. They are already conceding that there will be a whole new batch of minor changes to look into or, more seriously, big mistakes. (And that's apart from the biggest mistake of all… paying these people to waste their time and mine.)

As I understand it, mistakes against me – ie that lessen any of the payments I receive – will be my tough luck (unless I notice them and get them put right pronto). Meanwhile, mistakes in my favour won't benefit me unless, of course, I notice them as well and put in fraudulent claims!

Doesn't seem right, does it? Poor Alison is going to have to spend many dreary hours poring over the field numbers… again. This has been going on repeatedly now for about 15 years, and it really is time they were pulled up.

Onwards. There have been, as I'm sure you're aware, some rather regrettable incidents of walkers being trampled by cattle recently. Members of the public have been exercising their legal right to walk across farmland, almost always with dogs at their side, and some have been attacked by the cattle grazing this land. This is all very unfortunate, but hardly a new phenomenon. Things, however, are progressing of late. Increasingly it is being seen as the farmer's fault, to the point where one poor bloke is being sued for a very big sum.

Let's step back from this, shall we. Over recent decades the public have demanded, and been granted, increasing access to the countryside, but now find the business ordinarily carried on therein is not to their liking, and wish to sue the occupants for going about their normal work. The rationale is that 'farmers' know that their cattle may react to walkers and dogs crossing their fields, and yet wantonly continue to depasture these dangerous animals. Surely they deserve to be sued?

Well I must dispute this perception, Horace.

Despite my repeated and consistent objection, something over two thirds of my farm is now subject to open access, along with the entire common. The herds of cattle I graze hereabouts are the very reason the public can walk across the land in the first place, but now, seemingly, come second to these uninvited guests.

I would very much like to discuss this matter with persons complaining, solicitors acting for them, and anyone else who looks at me in a funny way. I should add that I will be opening discussions with a cudgel and a bad attitude.

(I've had a testing month. Does it show?)

And lastly… The Met Office.

I don't blame them for the bad weather that has troubled my summer. That would manifestly be unreasonable. I do, however, take exception to their woefully poor forecasting accuracy. Several times we've based harvest decisions on their forecasts, with expensive and miserable consequences.

I'm sorry, but doesn't this crew cost millions to function, using satellites and super-computers, with their primary objective being to forecast the weather? I'd say they fall pretty far short of a satisfactory standard, and need their arses kicked in a big way. Perhaps they'd like to be paid on results? Get it wrong too often: lose your job, house and pension! (Just like in the 'real world'.)

I'm perplexed that anyone in the organisation has the front to try and predict 'climate change' over coming decades given that they are pretty abysmal in guessing what the weather will do tomorrow or the next day.

Meanwhile, we've now started taking harvest decisions by a show of hands around the breakfast table. It's a more reliable system, but falls down when there is a hung vote, and I cast the decider. Then it's still my fault when it goes belly up.

I'm now awaiting a knock on the door, revealing a family complaining they've been trampled by my cattle. (Cattle which, I should clearly state, I had no idea were dangerous in any way whatsoever.) He'll no doubt be a Met Office employee; his good lady wife will be someone high up in 'mapping'. Their walking companion will be a 'no win no fee' solicitor.

Ha... I'll be waiting, cudgel in hand.

(As the door creaks open they'll realise, far too late, that the stampeding cattle were the least of their problems.)

OFFICIAL INMATE STATIONERY
WINDSWORTH PRISON
LONDON

Dear Roy

I got your postcard from Kew Gardens, thanks.

I came straight up with the Land Rover loaded with chainsaws, like you said.

When I arrived, I couldn't find you, so I went on, on me tod. Getting the Land Rover through the turnstile was a bit tricky, but I had the big bolt-croppers with me (the '3-foot universal key' as Chris calls them), so I was soon in the back gate over by the Chinese pagoda. (Sorry about the chain and padlock mate.)

I couldn't see which trees were marked to come out, so I guessed that it was the unmarked ones that were coming down. That was all of 'em back towards the big greenhouse for a start, which was going to take all day. I thought I'd better crack on.

As I taped off a clear area under that first row a few picnickers got uppity. I told 'em to sod off, and that Roy had told me it was OK. They went off in a huff.

Mind you, there were hundreds of others mooching about, so I put up some triangle signs as well. Don't know how we're expected to work with so many blinking people loafing about.

Anyway, I got right on. I dropped the first couple, thinking we could clean 'em up when you rocked up. Just as I was putting the back cut in the third – a gurt great stick of London plane – some geezer in a peaked cap came trotting down the path. Well, I waved and shouted, but he'd come under the tape while me back was turned. What else could I do?

That old plane hit him like a sledgehammer. He'd been shouting something as he ran, but the big Husky was running, and I had me ear defenders on, so I didn't catch it.

Well, what can I say? 250 cube had squat him flat as a dab.

I reached in under, and felt his pulse, but there wasn't one.

I realise now I should've stopped there and then, but the big saw is a bugger to start when it's hot, so I reckoned I'd better do a few more while it was running. I mean, matey was obviously a goner anyway, and until Chris rolled in, we'd never lift that stick off him. (Possibly, if you had the winch, we could've dragged it off of him, but well, he'd smear a bit wouldn't he?)

The next couple went over without too much fuss. The spindly acacia did catch a stupid spaniel that ran into the line of fire, chasing after a frisbee, but I never liked spaniels anyway.

I was pretty chuffed (apart from the spaniel, and the bloke in the peaked cap). I soon had 10 good sticks on the deck, then it all got a bit difficult.

Just as I was putting the dip in no. 11 (that really tall cedar, last in the row before the big greenhouse-type building) the wind changed. Well I tried to compensate, but once the dip was in I was committed. As the back cut got deeper, the wind took that old cedar, and as she went she twisted about half a turn the wrong way – away from me, luckily.

I've always said, if they let 'em get too big, too near the greenhouse, it'll end in tears. Sure enough, the top 30 foot of the cedar just 'clipped' the last bay of the greenhouse. What a din! You never heard such a tinkly crashing row.

A load of people came rushing out of the next door along, and a little golf-buggy-type cart, with a couple more of those blokes in peaked caps, came buzzing up the track. It was followed by a cop car with the lights and sirens going.

Well I put the saw down, but as I'd stood up straight again it seems someone tried to rugby tackle me. Look, it wasn't my fault; he come at me unawares, didn't 'ee?

When the hook of me felling bar caught him in the left nostril he kind of lost interest in wrestling me, but then the cops and two of the gardener types all piled in, and down I went. They seemed pretty excited about it all.

Anyway, to cut a long story short I'm now on remand, up before the beak next month for various offences, and I wondered if you could see your way to fronting me 20 grand for a lawyer. I did show your postcard to the lawyer they lent me, but 'ee doesn't think it constitutes a felling contract, and is refusing to act for me.

Alternatively, I been watching the guard shifts here, and reckon we'd have time to bust me out.

If you and Chris were ready with the Foden, and a long rope, parked halfway along the western wall at 4.05am on a Tuesday or a Thursday, we'd have about 15 minutes to get me over the wire. All you'd have to do is dangle the crane over the fence with the length of rope hanging down, and I'll grab hold. (I'd be grateful if one of you could throw a choke chain over the razor wires first, coz they buzz a bit in the wet. I think they'm charged up, an' it'd be better if they were shorted out.)

Perhaps Chris could backload with some of the sticks I knocked over in Kew? Save a bit of diesel wouldn't it. Mind, do tell him not to move that plane. I don't think anyone's realised that bloke is under it, and he might be a bit high by now.

I'll be waiting by the western wall, Tuesdays and Thursdays.

Egbert (C9999999)

Waiting for the sun

As the rain keeps battering against the west-facing windows, the mowing grass looks sadder and sadder. We did get a few hundred bales done before the monsoon began, but it was just too early to really motor on up here.

I am mindful of how technology has changed our lives though. I know I can, when I've really had enough, contract out the harvesting of this stuff on a single dry day to someone with the gear to handle wet grass. Just a few dry hours, and we'll have it. I'm not there yet, but we're close. Wet stinky silage is hardly what we want, but I don't intend to let it run on like last August and September.

Whenever I've been off the moor on a jaunt, from mid-July onwards, I've been seeing in-country fields of barley cleared on days when the dew could hardly have lifted. The driers must've been going overtime, or perhaps the crop ensiled somehow… and as for the straw! I suspect those men, like me, are not wanting to get caught again.

Where I'm going with this – and there is a point – is that at least we've got options nowadays.

History is sprinkled with records of periods like this, when some tract of Northern Europe or other endured successive years of wet and difficult summers. The periods were known as 'famines', and men and beasts perished in their droves. Now, we generally only think of 'famines' as drought related, but the word traditionally relates to events with other causes as well.

I find it sobering in the extreme to remember that in days of yore, before baled silage and corn driers, when shiploads of Brazilian soya beans weren't at the end of a phone, conditions like we've enjoyed recently would have seen the population of Europe thinned out in a fairly dramatic way.

Remember it's only these advances that permitted populations to spiral out of balance in the first place.

Anyway. I'm sat waiting. The shearing is done – with an expensive scab treatment in a group, due to a single ewe belonging to a neighbour. I really wasn't very happy about that. The blue tongue jabs are pretty much dealt with, and the Galloways bulled and about to go back on the hill.

The only way I can be sure of getting on with the harvest now, I've decided, is to go away on holiday. So I've booked a log cabin, in Scotland, for a week in August when I'd normally be hereabouts. You watch. It'll work like a charm.

Something I watched with dismay, again this summer, was the bloom wash off the spring calves through late July, as weeks of gales and rain took their toll. My only consolation is that it doesn't seem to be stopping the cows from breeding, and at least the yearlings respond once they're weaned and away to keep. Ho-hum.

The shearing is done

I recently hosted a farm walk for some sheep breeders from parts distant. A very convivial minibus full of them came down, visiting a couple of more, um, 'grown-up' Dartmoor farmers, as well as 'Haphazard Coaker'.

After they'd gone, I realised we'd experienced a cultural difference. Someone in their group noticed a bunch of my tups had slipped the net, and were grazing away in the valley, amongst ewes. 'Oh, you got the tups in?' No I explained, they had just ducked through an open gate, and I'd get them back directly. I realised later that the visitors had little grasp that Scotch or Cheviot ewes, on the peat, simply won't cycle in the summer, so the tups can escape all they like.

My old man reckoned to fetch the rams in by 1 September, although I've often had escapees do no harm until mid-September. Strange really, as the Cheviots will be looking for the tup just a few weeks later, but almost none will go on early.

Interesting difference I thought.

Right, I've got to get on with waiting for the weather again.

Holiday souvenirs

The record seems to be stuck again.

A prolonged monsoon season has curtailed my summer enjoyment once more, with the pattern becoming all too clear. There's a good week or three at midsummer, when I haven't got any grass to cut, then down it comes.

Alison and I did get the kids away for a week. Back to Dumfries and Galloway again this year. Same deal, we spent a week watching the Scots struggling in the weather, instead of cursing our own luck at home.

We had been waiting several days for one bloke to pick up a big area of grass, cut on lovely valley flats by Dalbeattie. Finally, one morning, a load of it was cleared at last. Sadly, it was cleared by a colossal flood that washed the lower half of the crop away in the night. There it was, strewn over the trees ½ mile downstream. Poor bugger, whoever he was.

Coakers on holiday

The lack of sheep on the higher ground, both in the Southern Uplands, and in the Lake District where we sneaked through en route, is blatant now. The majority of the ewes we saw were crossbreds, thinly spread on the lower and better pasture. Good lambs, for sure, but the soft option. The difficult ground is being abandoned like I've never seen before. Bracken spreads across vast tracts of grazing land.

On both upland and lowland I only saw two drainage crews at work the entire length of the western side of the country. Everywhere, blocks of lowland ground were abandoned to ragwort or pony paddocks – or both together in that happy union we know and love. Anywhere they still cared, toppers were keeping the vegetation down.

The majority of new infrastructure I did notice through middle England was on colossal amalgamated dairy units, where we didn't see the cows because they're all living inside now. Admittedly, there were still a lot of medium-sized Scottish dairy farms in evidence, but on many of those you can taste the lack of spending.

All in all this is a rather different picture to the one painted by Mr Benn* recently.

Now he has finally come out and told the world that he has discovered where food comes from, and that the cupboard is a bit bare, HB is personally going to redress the balance. No sh*t!

I am of course mightily glad to hear him begin to utter the awful news, but the bit of empty rhetoric is a long way away from telling us that what we do is vital to the stability of the social fabric that humanity relies on. I still get the feeling that 'we' are an ill-educated bunch of subsidy junkies, who'd rather be eating raw fox cubs than working, and who're not to be trusted. Policy at the coalface is still carping on about saving the butterflies, and sustainability.

Get this straight buddy, unless you're planning to cull millions, the human footprint is about as far from sustainable as it is possible to imagine. Your empty words about increasing homegrown food production are just a concession that there is a problem.

Sorry folks, that just kind of slipped out.

*I suppose we ought to touch on the idea that old Hilary might be waiting, like the 'Mr Benn' I recall from my childhood, for a little man to appear, and invite him back through a door to the reassuring old costume shop whereupon he can resume his normal life, with just some curio as a souvenir of his exotic travels.

What souvenir will Hilary be taking I wonder? A badger bite and a dose of bovine TB perhaps.

To redress things, I have to admit that I did secure a souvenir of my own recent journey, and purchased a little black Galloway heifer. Her dam is the most gorgeous Riggit cow in Christendom; and her sire an AI black bull from the sixties, built when they really knew how to build a bullock. Better than a kiss-me-quick hat, you've got to admit.

A holiday souvenir heifer

Autumn 2009

Mobile phone etiquette

I notice it is becoming commonplace for meetings/gatherings to be opened with a request to 'turn off your mobile phones please'. (This request is sometimes made rather firmer than a gentle suggestion.)

Obviously, being a hick who rarely uses such a tool* (and living where there is little reception for one anyway) I realise I'm behind those of you who have grappled with these issues. Etiquette of mobile phone use in mixed company is finding its place, although I have yet to get the hang of such niceties. Some common sense is universal though.

An instance. When listening to a guest speaker at an outing backalong, a local lad's phone went off. Now, in any instance, forgetting to turn your phone off, or to mute or something, in such a situation, is a bit of a cock-up. In this case, however, when the speaker was an interesting quietly spoken man who'd travelled 350 miles to share his wisdom with the assembly, having a phone ring during his talk was pretty poor form. The fact that the clown then answered it and started having a conversation... toe curling. (He very quickly got a different 'message' from those present.)

We do own a mobile telephonic device. I recently recognised an African tribesman, in the bush on a TV wildlife show, using the exact same model.

Weddings and funerals are another high-risk zone for offence. When young Jimmer got wed backalong I noted his family first wrestled him to the ground, and surgically removed his phone.

And I'd strongly advise you against interrupting a conversation to my face to answer your cell phone, putting me on hold by turning your head away, leaving a finger pointed at my nose. Trust me on this brother, when you turn back I'll either be gone, or you'll wish I was.

The other big field of dubious phone usage behaviour is, of course, that of what to do while driving.

You'll all know the issues, and you're probably still seeing, like me, plenty of vehicles whistling down the M5, driver with phone in hand.

Whilst on our travels last month we met the pinnacle of this brand of lunacy. A transit coming towards us, on a reasonably fast A road, was being piloted by a gibbon holding one phone to his ear with a shoulder, whilst holding another similar device with one hand, and tapping buttons on it with his 'spare' hand. (The only contact he had with the tiller was via one elbow.)

I was thankful we got past, but fully expected to hear 'Sally Traffic' telling us about the fallout from the inevitable moment he removed himself from the gene pool.

And speaking of Radio 2 (as we nearly were), what on earth is Terry Wogan going to get up to twixt now and when he pushes off? Will he ever get to retirement before he stretches the envelope just too far?

It was only recently, while feeding the cows in a tractor blessed with a wireless, that I realised what a card he is. He's been gabbling away forever, and it had never occurred to me that some of the material was a touch risqué. Then I started to listen a bit more attentively (I think I migrated to Radio 2 with Steve Wright, if that dates me accurately), and holy moly!

How he gets to the end of the 'Janet and John' stories is a mystery, and how he hasn't been taken off the air for them is another. I suppose, to be fair, I never cottoned on when I was a tacker, and therein lies Tel's defence.

His abilities are a very different kettle of teapots from those of his replacement, and I will miss him.

Bob Dylan and the Wurzels

Instead of pondering how to raise our food production to meet increasing population, and how this increase can be funded before escalating prices create general panic, I'm beginning to wonder if we'd simply be better found investing more in the MoD and setting them along the south coast.

I mean, I'm sure our servicemen are gainfully employed in Afghanistan – poor blighters – but meantime I understand there's a lot of Afghanis amongst the illegals camped at Calais, waiting for a lift over to easy street.

Wouldn't it soon be more appropriate to station those troops at Dover? If there are to be overseas duties, won't it be more pertinent to offer a couple of battalions to the Italians, to watch their coasts?

You think I'm kidding? Not altogether, I'm afraid. We won't be wringing our hands and asking how we can help the unenlightened join our system of Western democracy forever. At some point we'll be asking instead how we can stop them simply joining our Western populations.

A scary and sobering line of thought, which seemed fanciful not long ago, but will very evidently be pertinent to our sons. If this makes you call me a racist, I suppose you'll have to, but do get over that and ask how you will view things when the resources will no longer go round?

Isn't it better to have the factual debate now, before we're prompted to more knee-jerk reactions?

Anyroad. What's occurring hereabouts? Well, once harvest was put to beddy-byes, and the first mob of stores sold, Barry and I trucked off to demonstrate our mobile sawmilling★ ability at a woodfair in Dorset (or it might've been Wilts, or maybe Hampshire – I just followed signs off the A303 somewhere near Shaftsbury very early one Saturday morning).

★ *To be quite frank, while Barry demonstrates his sawing skills I exercise my best barrow-boy patter, and flog as much timber as is humanly possible in a 48-hour period.*

This salubrious event was held on a beautiful site up on Cranborne Chase's rolling downs, peopled by a charming crowd of visitors, and kindly organised by some very thoughtful souls. By thoughtful, I mean that as well as organising such a good show they had kindly laid on a band in the beer tent on Saturday night. So, at Beer O'clock, when the first day's punters had gone home, we could down tools and kick back and relax. The band played an eclectic range of tunes from old blues stuff, through a bit of skiffle, some zydeco, the odd Chuck Berry and Bob Dylan song, somehow finding their way to some Wurzels.

I'm generally not that comfortable up on the chalk, it having been settled by a tribe quite different to my own, but, happily enough, after the third or fourth mug of foaming ale it all made perfect sense (I'm told the chalk spring water adds to the ale immeasurably, and wouldn't argue).

Barry had dropped out by the time a Polish lad and I tried a bit of 'sing-along-a-Wurzels' (don't tell I tell 'ee, that's my philosophy), and I eventually kipped under a Galloway hide rug in the cab of the truck, and felt none the worse for it!

I wasn't quite as bright Sunday morning, but we still had a good weekend.

Back home again a mess of sheep tasks awaits, and the sawmill phone has been ringing off the hook.

CAT kills dog!!

Two of the small Coakers have been off on a skool trip to visit the local dump. No, sorry, landfill site – or do I mean the recycling centre?

Anyway, they've been shown all the clever ways the borough deals with the garbage we chuck in the bin. The staff went out of their way to explain all the processes involved, and to help the kids remember how much all this recycling costs, and the huge environmental impact waste has, then sent them home with reams of leaflets on the subject. John on one day, then Polly the next, both with another bag full of identical leaflets.

Hmm, I think I see a flaw in the plan there.

Meanwhile, on a parallel track running in the opposite direction, I note that Forest Enterprise (the 'Commission' to you and I) are endeavouring, through the use of emails, to attain the paperless office. This is the first time in some years I've witnessed them trying to fulfil their primary obligation – to maintain a strategic timber reserve – but one suspects it isn't quite the method their founders envisaged.

Given that some estates generously leased vast tracts of land to the nation for very specific reasons, I have speculated of late whether some of those estates are questioning current policy.

And drifting along with the literary current, I would also like to draw your attention to a simple sign that there is something fundamentally wrong with current FE direction.

As you know, English oak is our benchmark hardwood timber. It could hardly have played a bigger role in our nation's past, is the key component in many of our most precious native woodlands, and remains our best alternative to tropical hardwood. Currently though, oak woodland does have some issues. There are various environmental problems, mostly to do with warmer winters and airborne pollution, but more insidious is the steady ingress of Turkey oak volunteers. The wretched things hybridise all over the place, often spreading from specimen trees beside big houses. The Turkey is a vigorous tree, but has no commercial value – the reason being it rots – and had Henry VIII made his navy out of it we'd be *parlez*-ing *franglais* by now. Obviously, I avoid purchasing it as infeed for the mill, and groan when I see it creeping into native oak woodland, messing up the lovely diversity that exists in our native oak stock.

And where might you easily see examples of this steady encroachment, in amongst native oak volunteers? Why, right outside the FE offices at the top of Haldon. Staff have even thinned out some snarly looking saplings, to leave the upright straight stems to grow on. (Guess which ones are culled, and which are left?)

This is hardly a good sign, is it?

Moving right along, we've been greatly tickled by an ad seen locally of late, from a lady who claims to be able to put you in touch with your dead pet.

When we'd stopped laughing – we'd already long doubted the individual's integrity – we started to ask ourselves what exactly our long-dead pets might have to say?

'I'm very happy here, there's postmen's ankles on tap', or more likely 'Where are me nadgers, you sod? I thought I'd be reunited with them.' (To save me some time, please make up some more yourself.) I suppose if you're stupid enough to believe this line of tosh then you're a lawful and legitimate target for such nonsense.

And on the subject of deceased pets I have to tell you about the sad demise of a favourite collie backalong.

'Rip' was getting very doddery in her mid teens. She'd been my top dog for several years, but had long passed being able to work. She wobbled blissfully about the yard in her dotage, dribbling gently on passers-by who stopped to say hello, and barking at empty spaces for reasons unknown. She couldn't see too well, and could only hear me when she was close enough to lip-read.

Now we all know how this tale is likely to end, and luckily it was me at the wheel of a large piece of plant when it finally happened. (It was the CAT telehandler as it happens. Headline reads… 'Cat kills dog!'). I jumped out when I heard the yelp, and found her drawing her last gasp. I bent to pick her up, and her reaction was to bite the first thing she could reach. Yes, she died with my fingers clamped firmly in her remaining gnashers, and I have to advise you that this is not something you want to try if you can avoid it.

I wonder… did she go to doggy heaven, having passed away whilst biting the hand that fed her?

Curiouser and curiouser.

An exchange of medieval emails

This invite came in the post one autumn day, and is reproduced here by kind permission of the hosts, to make sense of the reply and follow-up they subsequently received.

Dear Friends, You are most warmly welcomed to a night of medieval merriment, **at Lower Merripit Farm, Dartmoor,** ON SATURDAY THE EIGHTH OF NOVEMBER **verily it starts at Half past Seven,** *celebrating the attainment of a half-century by the mistress of the house,* WITH RARE & WONDROUS VISITING MINSTRELS & BARDS (*Daughters of Elvin, Doublethead and The Roving Rivenstone Players*), Traditional Pie & Gravy Supper with Assorted Sweet Pastries & exotic oranges, WASSAIL BAR WITH VARIOUS ALES & CIDERS, *merry capering in the dance pavilion!* **genteel amusement in the old barn!** CULTURED WIT AT THE HEARTH FIRE! Period costumery is not absolutely obligatory *but thick worsted hose, rural bodkins, leather snoddies and warm jerkins are thoroughly recommended, for indeed the night may be cold,* FORSOOTH! BRING FORTH A GOODLY BOTTLE FOR THE WASSAIL BAR, **and hark! share with the gathered company your** chivalrous tales of daring-do, *juggling & tumbling acceptable but not encouraged,* **stabling and hostelry available in adjacent cottage,** BRING YOUR OWN BEDDINGS, **it may be cosy,** VERRILY WE AWAIT YOUR REPLY *with our warmest regards N. Shaw (squire) and C. Hillyer (wyffe).*

One response they received ran as follows:

My dearest Baron Merrimentpit
Verily, we are mightily tickled by your invitation, and would find it hard to decline. I humbly draw your attention to a mistake on the part of your scribe. He suggests the festivities celebrate the

attaining, by the Mistress* of the house, of a half century. Surely he has pre-empted this illustrious event by some years. I've no doubt that he will be languishing in your dungeon by the time my messenger safely brings this reply. I shall surely assist with the tongs when we next are met. I find one more turn of the screw, once the wrenching sound finally desists, is usually sufficient to hold their attention.

*I have hitherto been under the impression that the word Mistress comes neatly twixt Mister and Mattress, but you may soon disabuse me of this theorem.

I remain concerned that my snoddies might not be leathern enough, although a warm jerkin is widely forsooth to be a sound beginning to the eventide! The concept of wearing a bodkin confounds, as I understand it to be a slim piercing projectile for defeating a chain mail shirt (is it not justly observed that the way to a man's heart is just under his fourth rib?). I will do my uttermost.

Do you need some filling for the pie? Should rat-tails run short, I would be honoured to send an envoy with some fatted oxen. My ploughman assures me a fine Galway ox of the banded type awaits the steel.

I hearken to your call for additional wassailing flasks, and may have to try and amaze you with the recent invention of some Celt and Gael tribes, who have discovered the technique of boiling their wine, cider or, better still, their malted barley ale, and catching the resultant humours.

The coppersmiths* of the central sea have helped them in this process, and their produce is widely referred to, in their heathen tongue, as 'the water of life'. Its consumption on my part may well allow your jester to have an evening's rest. In fact, I shall makest apology at this advance stage for any performance of mine which may cause offence to yourselves, your honoured guests, or more especially, the buxom serving wenches whom I sincerely hope will once again be on hand to lend assistance to an elderly squire such as myself.

I hope and trust that the quality of these wenches will be of your usual high standard, and their forbearance of frail and emotional gentlefolk such as ourselves will match previous visits to your lands. A sound scolding should be all they need to administer, should my attentions become most unwelcome.

*A little piece of Kipling for you, Sire.
   'Gold for the Mistress
   Silver for the maid.

Copper for the craftsman, cunning in his trade.
"Good!" said the Baron, sitting in his hall, "but it's iron, cold iron that's the master of them all."'

My wyffe, the fair maid Allyson de Worcester Parke, looketh forward to enjoying your bounteous hospitality on that evening.

Our palfrey, thank you for your offer of stabling, will be perfectly at rest out of doors, and needs no fodder during the night. (It survives on an essence we have to secure from traders from deepest Arabia.)

I must away to thrash my serfs.

I beg leave to remain your humble servant
Jarl Anton of Sherberton

And, after the event, a letter of thanks to the Good Baron:

My Honourable Baron Merrimentpit, and the fair Lady Carolyn
As long we suspected, your revelries proved most illustrious, rewarding and informative.

My good Lady and I enjoyed ample quantities of all the resplendent and fulsome victuals offered. I do so hope that none of your impressive and genteel guests suffered from a 'surfeit of lampreys', and indeed I am pleasantly impressed that one might survive one eventide without consuming any flesh whatsoever. This was a revelation to us.

I should say that the volume of plant matter I enjoyed has given rise to ever more gross humours than I am used to, but readily concede that these humours may be akin to those brought about by an over-indulgence in the medieval elixir my flagon contained.

Verily, many partook of this elixir; oft finding it gave them warmth within that they had hitherto not experienced. Sadly I cannot reveal the formula, given that the secret was entrusted to me by the Abbot of an ancient order, whose novices Brother Jack and Brother Daniel had been preparing the main ingredient of this potion in a small cloister in the distant hamlet of Lynchburg, Tennessee (pop. 247).★
★The Baron will be enchanted to hear that I once knew a fair maid who christened her first born with those two names (Jack and Daniel). I never fully ascertained whether a critical, and initial moment in the infant's existence was influenced by these monikers.

I could dwell on my recollections of the fair maid, and her two equally fair sisters, all of whom rode fiery iron steeds cunningly fabricated by skilled smiths and artisans, but, perhaps, I should not.

As we expected, the quality of your troubadours remains as exulted and elevated as any travel-worn guest would desire, although the storm that bleweth suggests your priest needs to apply more vigour to his study of the relics.

And the alliance of the weather and my fair Allyson's desire to bring along her mighty hound would only have led to merry witticisms regarding 'not putting a knight out on a dog like this', so we'll remove the narrative hence.

Oh, and Allyson has firmly instructed me to convey her sincerest gratitude. Although her responsibility for the safe return of our palfrey precluded her partaking of excessive liquid refreshment, it did mean she remained able to restrain her master as he became increasingly emotional during the latter stages of the eventide. He would doubtless otherwise have developed an unhealthy interest in your very fine supply of wenches, and hopes his thus greatly reduced licence caused no offence. Certainly, no slur was intended upon your wenches. (I do readily admit that my inability to recall my actions oft relates directly to the strength and volume of the refreshment I have enjoyed, and the calibre of actions needing recollection. Perhaps his Baronship has noticed the phenomenon himself?

I remain your humble servant
Jarl Anton of Sherberton

Eating Galloways

Pulling the cows together for autumnal jobs and starting to throw some grub about has shown a crop of quite respectable calves, despite the miserable summer. A few have evidently made heavy weather of it all, but most of the cattle have thrived.

A bunch of South Devon steers sold quite well, considering they'd spent almost all their six months on damp black peat soil at 1100 feet. Some of the spring-born Galloway calves were comparatively better, despite having been in rain clouds around 1400 feet most of their lives. I won't be selling them as suckled calves, except one or two hotly sought Riggit breeders and a show beast or two, so I can take my choice of replacements. We're building up pedigreed heifers as fast as we can for HLS purposes. (Hardly a good reason, but hey-ho. I can see which way the wind blows.)

The Galloway boys will mostly be headed for our own, and other, specialist beef rounds.

I haven't really got to grips with being able to run them to a better age yet, given that they're best taken through to three to four years. The funny thing is, despite the howls of derision I can hear echoing up the valley, and knowing that they could be pushed on faster – plenty of Galloway bull calves have been corned to slaughter weight in 14–15 months – I know the best beef will come from steers skidded about on fuzz and rocks for another couple of years. Several customers have recently phoned, raving how fantastic the last steer is eating, and I promise you he'd been running on one of the poorest newtakes we've got, eating molinia grass, whortleberry and gorse.

A recent conversation with a pal at the bar of 'The Ferrets Rest' revealed that he and his brothers – beefy old boys who know how to live, and who have bred and reared thousands of cattle out on the hill – keep Galloway steers, for their own consumption, until they're five years old. Now what does that tell you?

Conversely, men who should know a lot better have been wasting some time recently trying to impress on me how fattening cattle is such a specialist job, and how they must be fed just so, to exactly this weight, and have exactly that confirmation.

I tried to explain that I'd killed – and helped eat – something over 100 Galloway steers so far this millennia, and not a damned one of them was to a size and shape that Sainsco's man would've touched. And yet... well, most of my customers, and the family, can no longer eat beef 'out' for fear of disappointment.

Sadly these blokes have been brainwashed. Whilst they understood the words I used, the key element of my response went right past 'em. Never mind.

Last week, as a group of us downed tools and repaired to the kitchen for a warm up and a bite to eat, I recalled that I'd scoffed the last of the bread earlier. Hmm, I wasn't sure what we'd find. Beans without toast perchance. (Doesn't feel right, does it?)

Anyway, what we actually found was two loaves baking in the Aga, courtesy of my 10-year-old boy. What a star! He'd heard his mother grumbling that she'd forgotten bread, and had quietly rectified the situation.

The lads and I decided that, while we might've had better bread, it had seldom been as welcome, and the first loaf soon disappeared. Mind, when the boy noticed this, he took umbrage. (I don't think he even saw a slice from that one.) So he hid the other one, in case it went the same way.

Now I don't want you to run away with the idea that the sun rises and sets on him. He is a difficult little sod at times, and as testy as the best of 'em when crossed. I'm not sure how many of us it'll take to hold him down to get his hair cut, for instance, although the promise of a trip to a rare poultry auction has raised the concept of a compromise in this department.

And finally, it is with a heavy heart I have to report the unexpected departure of my dear friend Jonathan Seward.

Jonathan was an understated character, who somehow gave the impression of being so relaxed and easy-going that you'd never guess how much work he actually got through, or how well he farmed. He took all of life's troubles in his steady stride, and yet still found time to smell the roses and have some fun along the way. Everyone he met on life's highway was touched by his down-to-earth and generous open nature.

To me Jonathan was the best of company when things were rolling along OK, but stood out most when things went pear shaped. He proved the most reliable stalwart when the storm clouds gathered in 2001, the kind of friend a man needs.

He added colour to our lives with his gentle humour and dry observations.

He's been one of the pillars of that quiet rural community which is almost invisible to most of modern Britain, yet which remains the unsung backbone of so much that we hold dear.

Jonathan leaves a lovely family, and a huge hole in all our lives. So long mate. I'm so very sad that you were taken so soon, but equally glad that I counted you a friend.

Winter 2009/2010

Hot news. Wood burns!

As the nice radio lady précised the newspapers for me this morning, something caught my attention. I quote: 'Gordon Brown is to be told today…' (something to do with the MoD, and how many helicopters they can't buy/bring into service 10 years after buying/keep in the air). Now if Gordie listens to the same radio station, or reads whichever paper was being reviewed, then he'd already know, and therefore wouldn't need telling. Hmm, does he then have to look interested, keeping up the pretence?

Anyway, on general principles I think Gordon should 'be told' whenever anyone gets the chance.

Meanwhile, I hear my pal Colin's boy has been doing a spot of spear fishing. Backalong he proudly came back with a whacking great sea bass. Now even I know these are about the best eating fish found off our shores, and much sought. Colin was delighted – practically tucking a napkin under his collar as he turned up the grill. Sadly for Colin, Will also knew how much the fish was worth in town, and slipped out the door pretty smart. I hear all Colin saw was one little fillet eventually sent back for Dad.

Like me, I suspect a mess of DEFRA policy and news items has been vexing you of late. I'm trying to put them all together in one succinct humorous story, but failing.

The key ingredients of the broth include the electro-tagging of my moth-eaten hill ewes, the concerted attack on cattle keeping and meat eating by some rather trendy (but short-sighted and unrealistic) bozos whilst stating I must produce more provender, and the insane DEFRA decision to remap all British farmland again.

Then there's the revelation that if we plant half the country with trees, we could fuel about 22 houses with woodchips.* Meanwhile, thousands can go on flying to the Canaries for some winter sun with abandon, and the prospect of some union action fills the nation with outrage. In the next newscast there are compelling suggestions that vast tracts of arable land are about to go under the rising sea levels, or get blow away in continent-wide dustbowls.

Simplest if I give you a brief snapshot into our lifestyle on rain-lashed Dartmoor, and you can see for yourselves why I can't quite make sense of it all.

Through the late autumn, as the lads and I hunted down the sheep on the common for dipping and tupping, fielding the last lamb as it swept down a waist-deep torrent just on dusk, then started fetching in the hill cows, weaning and housing what needs shelter from the howling gales prevalent hereabouts, Alison was struggling to check the myriad changes to the hundreds of 'enclosures' on our maps again. (Mind she's done this several times in the last decade.)

One block of 220 acres, fenced and run as one enclosure, and through which all the above stock work ebbs and flows, includes several ruined farmsteads/cottages from centuries past, when a man could raise a family on four or five cows. The enclosure has a mile of river, various streams, Bronze Age boundaries, all marked and mapped, and masses of tin workings stretching over hundreds of years, many features of which the satellite is peculiarly interested in. There are bridlepaths, footpaths, a County Council road, a private driveway, sunken packhorse tracks, and ¾ mile of metalled water board track. Some acres are wide expanses of river valley bog, overlaid and in amongst the medieval tin-streaming works. Some are dense clitters of above-ground granite boulders as big as the Land Rover, lying next to an extensive scheduled ancient monument (12–15 hut circles). Leats, ditches, wheelpits and tin 'blowing houses' lie all about, and there are ridge-and-furrow systems. For good measure, there's a monastic apiary, in a walled-off softwood plantation.

And guess what? The satellite picks up nearly all of it, and wants to identify every damn piece separately. I merely want to run a few Scotch ewes and Galloway cows over it, and oh, our Dartmoor stallion keeps his harem on it.

My poor, poor Alison, however, has to make it fit all the forms.

She trumped the lot yesterday, when she discovered that, with the deadline looming, the office dealing with this hurried remapping lunacy were all off for their Christymas lunch – during normal office hours – and wouldn't be answering the phones for the rest of the day.

And you still wonder why I'm grizzly about all this?

Sorry, back to the revelation that you can heat your house by burning sticks, which nature then re-grows for you in a satisfyingly short carbon loop. My goodness, whatever will they discover next!

Well, I thought you'd be interested in some numbers. Houses we supply with enough sticks to really do some heating – as opposed to those who just like to look at a fire – get through something like 5–6 tonnes of firewood per winter. Now hereabouts, you'd be lucky, with professional levels of ongoing management, to grow that much – part dry debarked – volume per hectare annually (unless you're going to plant nasty Sitka spruce forests, or possibly eucalypt – and that's where my money is). That doesn't sound too bad does it, one hectare per house?

Now 60 million folk must be, what, 12 million+ households? Twelve million hectares would be about 29 million acres, or just OVER HALF the landmass of the UK.

I'm all in favour of the general principle, but I spot a problem here.

Dark days and long nights

On the face of it, contemplating winter hardly instils enthusiasm, does it?

The repetitive round of feeding chores I have alluded to before, the constant rain and muddy tide marks halfway up your trouser leg, just at the top of the welly boot line★ – and if you think that's a bother, ask the girls about the 'welly boot stubble line' which lurks beneath those trouser legs!

★A kind of rural version of the Plimsoll line, being the depth to which you can sink in the slurry before you send out a mayday call – or a claim to Lloyds.

The morning routine will see one of us spending two to three hours in a tractor cab. It's generally me and my No. 1 collie dog. Our days – and, without serious scrubbing, our nights – will be seeped in an all-too-familiar whiff of damp silage, waterproofs and collies. Mix some bovine muck and sheep grease into the heady mix, and I wonder some perfume house isn't on the phone for the recipe!

A steady weeks' rain/sleet will see the leggings rarely properly dry, and likewise the favourite hat. Hardly surprisingly, hill farmers tend to have a balanced view on waterproof clothing. Whilst they want to remain as dry and cosy as possible, they are also aware that a super-duper designer brand name 'boretex' jacket has its limits. It will go down the Swanee just as quick as any other when it gets rubbed into the barbed-wire fence as a cow pushes past, or when a Scotch ram hooks his antler into the gusset. The real difference is the size of the price tag on the replacement.

In fact, as I have observed before – whilst stood on a freezing hillside with our pal Beryl, looking for an errant sheep as it happens – 'recreational walkers' and 'enthusiasts' are easy to tell from the bucolic yokels on winter hillsides.

The weekend warriors will surely be clad, as is their wont, in bright hews of boretex, designer scarves, and boots that cost more than the missing hog was worth. Their hats have to have the right label, and be colour co-ordinated, having been bought from a glossy catalogue – modelled by a chiselled smouldering bloke whose name is probably Dirk Strong. The telescopic walking pole has long since replaced the 'azel thumb stick.

Beryl and I meanwhile, knowing what to expect up there, were accordingly attired in multiple layers of whatever garments came to hand, and that would keep the cold out. I can't speak for my colleague, but my own fetching ensemble included a 20-year-old inherited overcoat, several Christmas presents, the gleanings from a jumble sale, a 'borrowed' hat, at least two pieces of baler twine, and a cut-off length of alkathene water pipe – the 'techno' replacement for the hazel stick. The overcoat had greatly suffered from the having the Scotch ram 'Git' hook an antler in it, as described above.

The colours of these ethnic outfits are generally fairly dull, so as not to startle the cattle, or the hungover. Occasional exceptions include a recent spate of fluorescent green safety coats which give me a headache just to think about, but they soon get scuffed back to non-dazzle intensity.

A further observation is, when the weekend has passed and the 'enthusiasts' have all gone home, the likes of Beryl and I are still to be found out there somewhere, doing what needs to be done… and when the chips are down, if you were a missing hogget, who would you want looking for you?

And why would we keep on doing it/going out in the cold and the wet?

Well, personally, I can say it has its benefits. For a start, I get to listen to the radio in peace between groups of cattle. The beasts rarely answer back, or demand a new computer game/sofa/frock/mountain bike (delete as appropriate). Admittedly they tend to kick if I sneak up behind them, but I'm sure we could stretch that metaphor if we tried.

And best of all? When everything is fed, and the sun dives below another winter's eve, I can retire to the fireside for a warming dram.

Good health!

Ravening ravens

As winter arrived with a bang, very punctually I thought, so various twits were waxing lyrical about how picturesque it all was. The snow-capped moors, and hoarfrost-adorned trees have been much photographed and admired. Kids were able to go sledging, and all must be well with the world. Hmm. Well up in the backwoods of said snow-capped moors tempers have been a bit frayed. The feed pipe to the water reservoir eventually freezes, and then we've got about 10 days until things go critical – and they have. We deliver sawn timber from the mill with a 7.5 tonne truck, backloading with things that won't otherwise fit over those quaint medieval bridges… I can no longer get deliveries of cattle cake, for instance. Well, the flatbed truck grips about as well as something that doesn't grip at all. It's OK loaded, but empty? Forget it. That's been a bit of an issue of late.

At least I had the foresight to order new batteries for several machines suspected of sluggardly cold-morning behaviour.

We hadn't finished getting youngstock moved from its autumn pastures before the glaciers formed on various local roads. And trust me buster, you don't want to be towing a stock box behind the Land Rover, over recent road conditions, when it's stuffed full of steaming 18-month-old bullocks.

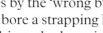

The run of winter calves by the 'wrong bull' was broken when a favourite old black cow bore a strapping heifer by the right bull, and beautifully marked into the bargain. We left her standing over her new baby, on a patch of grass amongst the snow, and went on to the next group. An hour later she'd wandered off and the ravens had pecked sodding great holes in the calf. (I generally love to see ravens about, and phlegmatically acknowledge that they've got to eat something… but I rather wish they'd found something else that particular morning.) I tried stitching it back together with hairs plucked from the tail of the wife's cob, but there seemed to be bits missing, and it didn't survive. M'own damn fault. Should've got them straight in, there and then. (The fact that the calf didn't jump straight up, and that the cow left it, suggests that something else was wrong with it – something other than the great gaping holes, that is.)

For good measure, what we'd thought was an oedema on the old cow transpired to be a gurt rupture, so she left the premises feet first very soon after. Ho-hum.

To date, the fodder looks like it will last fairly well, although I've been a bit hard thinning mouths out to start with. (A cow seen to be empty has to be pretty damned precious to avoid a one-way trip, outbound.) We're going to need a few round bales of insurance yet. What will happen to the spot price, should things continue as they started, I don't know. My gut feeling is that there's ample silage about, if the logistics can be made to work. I wouldn't hold out too much hope if you're looking for some nice conventional bales of hay though. A pal reports he's steadily selling his little bales to a merchant, for £5 each collected. His Dad is shaking his head, bemoaning that you shouldn't sell your hay off the farm. Given that their big crossbred cows would easily scoff one a day, and winter in that parish lasts something over 120 days… that'll be £600 in fodder per cow this winter then Dad?

Just before the weather kicked off we'd sensibly had the red diesel tank filled. It's a steel tank that's been propped on its granite perch as long as I can remember, which dates it a bit. The morning it was refilled I was the delegated refuelling monkey, juicing things up for a busy day. Stood filling a drum for Barry's saw, I noticed a drip from a bottom corner. Three seconds later, it had a friend. Hmm, said I. Tanker driver must've spilt a bit, and it's found its way down to the bottom edge. I went off with that drum, returned to fetch a drink for the old Browner that drives my saw, and realised I was watching a steady drip. Eek! Clutching at straws, I tried to think of any other explanation, but there simply wasn't one. I was just going to have to drain the whole lot. I subsequently filled every machine on the place brim full, and then went a'hunting spare drums, giving them a bit of a rinse and filling them up too. It took most of the day.

I suppose I'm grateful that when the old tank's day finally came it wasn't in a catastrophic manner, with all the attendance issues that would arise. Malc has put in a very smart new tank, in a bunded installation. Now, if only I could afford to fill it!

Lastly, I'll give you one more thought. Much in the news at the time of writing are recent student demonstrations, and how the law have responded. There was some twerp clambering ill-advisedly over the Cenotaph, and other twits relieving themselves against the statue of Winston Churchill – both pretty ironic, given how the freedom to so express your dissatisfaction has been protected in Britain. Why, even my landlord, HRH, got caught up in it, with the old limo being roughed up.

The thought that came to me was possibly the same one which came to you. How many countries in the world would have allowed the little morons to walk away from that? The fact that none of those demonstrators was shot on sight speaks volumes of our great nation. That only one head got cracked I find an extraordinary display of restraint and control.

Sadly, were you and I left in charge, we would no doubt be using the worst-behaved individuals as an abrupt example to others. I do realise that this would rather spoil things. Next time we're met, we'll compare strategies.

Crisp and bloody even

This entry might be a bit like despatches from the front, given that my world is deep frozen and covered in great drifts of 'global warming', but then I suspect that yours is as well. In fact, seeing Richard Betton feeding Swale ewes up over the back of the Pennines on the TV news reminded me how balmy it is down here. (Mind you, I'm suspicious how the TV crew got there. Ha! Caught you, Mr B.)

Let's look on the upside then, shall we?

- My outdoor cattle are making no mess whatsoever.
- The loader tractor has been coaxed into life every day so far, and the very cold crunchy snow has remained 4x4 drivable almost every day.
- I've managed to plough through the drifts in every gateway that I need to, and the water system has mostly held up, although the pump is on constant to keep the main feed moving once I'd got it liquid again.
- The lads have got here, in varying combinations, almost every day – Joby had to pedal halfway on his bike, with an overnight bag, knowing I was suffering with a cold, and feeding up on me tod over the weekend.
- There's precious few people turning up bothering me – one or two ramblers a week, no picnickers/dog walkers, and only a smattering of weekend 4x4 warriors – given away by the snorkel/huge tow rope/ tools strapped to the roof. And most of them soon crashed their stupid 'willy substitute' trucks into each other and went home nursing bent toys.

- The sawmill phone is very quiet.
- Most of the stock is absolutely fine, and best of all, most critically in my life… I can walk right up to the round feeders, and jump around with impudence, without any boot overflowing issues.
- There's 80 days' fodder in the heap.

The downside?

- The sawmill phone is very quiet. (Although Barry is struggling to make much headway with orders anyway. The logs are frozen into the heap, the dirt is frozen onto the logs, the stacked timber is stuck together, and the bandsaw lube has to live in the kitchen until 10 minutes before B needs it. This method works very well, but doesn't pass the 'Wife' approval test.)
- There's only about 80 days' fodder on site.

Walking home to the calving box *Joe Tanner (on his mobile)*

The South Devon cow found missing one morning chose to cross the Dart to go into labour, and did so on the morning the loader tractor had a flat foot.

This led to Barry and Malc having to shuttle tyresmith/ compressor/tractor to and from the main road, while Joe and I strode off Scott-like with fodder and ropes to find the cow.

When we got there she still hadn't delivered, and it looked like a calving aid job. Seeing as his tongue wasn't lolling out swollen, I decided that 'Fred' could stay where he was, tucked up in the warm, while Joe and I persuaded his Mum to get to her feet and walk home. As she stumbled through the river crossing with freezing torrents swirling up to her midriff I did wonder what we were going to do if she went down just then!

Anyroad, the old girl walked ¾ mile back to the yard where we put her to bed in a loosebox, and delivered her of a strapping great bull calf without further problems. Turned a frown into a smile! Anyway. What you really need to know is how many new types of snow we've identified. As you'll know, the Eskimo… Oh alright then, the Inuit if you must – given that 'Eskimo' is a derogatory (Cree?) term meaning 'eater of raw flesh' – well anyway, they have over 100 words for snow, no doubt including one which roughly translates as 'yellow snow' (and Frank Zappa says 'Don't you eat that yellow snow'*).

Well we've been enjoying 'the snow that sticks to your boots, then melts on the scullery floor, making your socks wet'. Then there are the balls of snow and cow crap, which slowly accumulate around the round feeders, like so many green boulders. There's the tongue of spindrift which slides gently up the drift and spills softly over the wall at the top of the lane in picturesque fashion, until the moment you get out of the tractor to shut the gate, when it gusts into a sandblasting knife of freezing agony, which is going scour yer eyeballs out of their sockets. There's the specially brewed sticky stuff which adheres to the branches of the beech trees around the yard, until you pass below and it can plummet down the back of your collar.

I'll stop now… I've had enough, and want to be lying on a tropical beach. A well-heeled retired couple down the road have battled off the moor to get to Southampton to catch their place on a four-month cruise, taking in all parts sunny. I gently probed to find out how big their largest suitcase was… 'Look, see, I can fold myself up really small.'

Back to Frank Zappa for a moment. I was hitchhiking through rural northern California one afternoon, 20 years ago, and discovered that the 1960s were very much alive and living in and around Humboldt County, in some kind of giant inverted time capsule.

A VW camper van chugged past, through the peculiar dusty yellow sunlight, sporting the bumper sticker 'Frank Zappa for President'. Well it tickled me, and given whom the Yanks have elected since I'm not so sure the hippy piloting the combi-van was so far off the mark. (I only tell you this snippet to warm us both up a bit.)

❧

Going for a mad tramp up on the moors

I must share with you a nuance of what I see from the hill.

Nowadays, the earnest walking brigade who tramp through my yard on their way to becoming lost and fogbound in some mire, wearing their bright hues of expensive 'boretex', clackety clack their way along using telescopic walking poles. Now you and I will cut a piece of hazel★ from the hedge, using our highly offensive weapon – sorry, pocket knife – or possibly we might grab a cut-off length of alkathene pipe, but they have all gone over to these techno-sticks.

★*I have to remember to cut hazel when I'm at lower altitudes, since it hardly grows here.*

Anyway, I have observed a couple of variations recently. First I met one of the urban re-settlers in the village clacking along… not with a telescopic pole, I was delighted to see, but with a bright blue plastic leccy fence stake (purchased to control the 12 hens in the back garden).

Next up was a couple of lads I passed the time of day with as they strode up the bridlepath. They were identified as 'walking enthusiasts' by their attire, but were leaning upon... wait for this… neatly hewn hazel thumbsticks! It seems to be some kind of retro-statement, a radical sign of flaming rambler youth, and it tickled me.

The lads also think very well of me now, I might add, as I discovered they were in fact headed 180 degrees in the wrong direction, and saved them a rather longer hike than they'd anticipated.

❧

And sorry, while still on hiking about in the fog. The editor of one publication for whom I scrawl recently told me she was 'going for a mad tramp up on the moors'.

I asked her later whether she'd had any luck and found one? Bless, she didn't catch my meaning at all. (And those of you suggesting she'd have been better off loitering about my yard can just sod off.)

❧

News filters out that Angelina and Brad may have split, and that she wants more kids (or maybe not, depending on which paper you're reading, and which day of the week it is). I'm insisting that the phone lines are kept clear just in case. I wouldn't want her to get a busy line when she calls.

(Alison scoffs, guffaws even, for reasons unknown.)

The sawmill is going hammer and tongs, although the snow backalong hampered various aspects. Barry battled in most days, but then had to remember what orders he'd cut yesterday because they were invariably lost in the drifts each morning.

Somehow, all the machinery started each day, although the jump leads have been out a fair bit. And firewood sales remain buoyant.

Ho-hum. Roll on spring.

Agnes and I were discussing mining over wheaties this morning (it has to be said, our Agnes has eclectic interests). I was explaining that the miners always used to prefer larch for pit props, because it 'talks' before it fails, giving everyone a chance to skedaddle before the roof falls in. Agnes was then able to start telling me why miners might want to keep a canary with them… 'Oh, I know this,' I stopped her, 'it's something to do with their not exploding when exposed to a naked flame.' Agnes roundly scolded me, so I tried suggesting it's because, in fact, canaries burn with a blue flame in the presence of some gas or other (although only a strain bred by famous canary breeder Mr Humphrey Davy of the 'Patent Davy Safety Canary' fame).

My daughter thinks I'm talking cobblers, but I'm sure I'm on the right trail.

OK, a gag to send you on your way.

Bob, a 'mature' bachelor farmer, went to the doctor for a check-up (having been avoiding the matter for some time).

Next market day his doctor saw the old fellow staggering through town with a gorgeous young woman on his arm. The girl was attired somewhat alluringly, the doctor considered, and Bob was looking decidedly rough.

'Hello Bob,' says the quack, 'this is a turn up. Everything OK?'

Farmer Bob, leaning equally on his horn head stick and the lass's arm, replies, 'Well I'm doin' me best boss, but I don't know how long I'll be able to keep this up.'

'What are you talking about Bob?'

'Well I'm following your instruction Doc. Yer told me… "You get a hot mamma and be cheerful."'

'No Bob,' says the doctor. 'What I said was… You've got a heart murmur. Be careful.'

Mmm, smeared in Marmite

With that special kind of 'beaurocrappic' pinched view of farmers, various arms of government have been bothering us of late.

Top of the list is the answerphone system in a department I can't name. My lovely Alison has had cause to ring this department to fulfil obligations under some scheme or regulation. Failure to comply will ultimately lead to my losing payments/being fined, which would make my farming business an unsupportable drag on my finances. Not wanting to be overdramatic, I would have to cease farming, potentially losing my agri-tenancy rights, and hence my family home.

Like many of you, we don't really have the choice but to deal with these people. Alison called the number, and got the 'press 3 if you want to strangle someone now' machine. She followed the trail, pressing the required sequence of numbers, until the machine cut her off, line dead. Not to be outdone she tried following a slightly different sequence, but was eventually dumped in the same manner (this is the telephonic equivalent of every corridor in the building leading you out the back door).

Now my wife is a determined woman – a couple of decades around me has probably helped – but she couldn't, no matter how she tried, get through to a real person, or an answerphone that took a message, on the main number. This was in an office with which we absolutely have to communicate.

Her mood was not especially good after half an hour (I haven't dared speculate whether this is some kind of premium rate line). And now I come to think of it, perhaps I might set up such a thing for incoming calls, and put the number on every form I fill in. Likewise, we'll transfer any rep/telesales Muppet who bothers me.

Remember, you owe me a drink when yours starts to work!

Now the news this morning told of a recently completed study which has revealed that, shockingly, rich people live longer than poorer. Likewise the 'well educated' live longer than the 'less well educated'.

Has it occurred to anyone that smarter people, taken as a whole, use their noggins to learn, and then earn more? Smarter people might very well then read in their broadsheet paper that eating sensibly, exercising a bit, and generally laying off the excess, will lengthen their lives.

It would be cruel but succinct to suggest that daft people live shorter lives than clever clogs. And what do you want me to do about this?

I know Tony and his pals ranted on about social mobility. Is this study somehow connected… 'It's a disgrace, the rich even live longer' (and isn't there some contradiction in Tony and Cherie's slavish devotion to personal wealth?).

In any case, a balanced view would hold that reading the redtop tabloid★ (or at least looking at the diary pages), wallowing in beer and fags, and gorging on fast food, might very well kill you quicker than nibbling carefully on a bit of muesli and living like a monk full of angst – but you may also find yourself a happier soul.

But hang on… If rational thought takes us back to reading the tabloid for the sake of… Oh, the conundrum!

Anyway, I think such studies are a monumental waste of time. You can't fix stupid, as they say, and the more you try and coddle those who can't work it out for themselves, the less likely you are to foster the utopian society you desire.

It has now come to the point in this 'socially mobile society' where, as dutiful parents wanting our kids to have the chance of further education, Alison and I are wandering if we shouldn't give up work. The effort we put into running our various businesses, struggling to better our lives just takes us further away from the 'under-privileged' who the government are so desperate to help into university.

Again, just seeing this irony probably condemns me in some way.

★*Sorry, back to the redtop tabloids. One freezing February morning I kindly took a cuppa in an enamel mug, and a couple of bits of toast, up to Barry in the mill (selfishly wanting him to keep going). The toast I folded into a couple of sheets of newspaper to keep warm. Being a thoughtful soul, I arranged the paper to reveal the page 3 daily diary picture as it was unfolded… for t'was a copy of* The Sun *another of the lads had left around. 'Mmm,' smiled Barry, as he unwrapped his toast, 'smeared in Marmite.'*

Now there's a thought.

Aston Martins and polo ponies

With an election pending, I've been listening to the bull-dust billowing from Westminster.

Now, Labour presided over the financial meltdown, and put us into debt forever, but hey! They're socialists… is it really reasonable to expect them to be able to run the financial sector?

And as far as I can understand these things, we've swapped colossal and ill-advised collective personal debts for an equivalent black hole on the public slate. I'm not too sure how this happened, and since I didn't have any debts at the outset of the debacle, but now I seem to have acquired my share, I rather think I've been done.

Is this the redistribution of 'wealth' that socialists keep banging on about?

Can't say as I like it very well.

In the other camp sits that 'man of the people'… cuddly Dave.

For goodness sake, he is an old Etonian and Oxbridge scholar, and comes to the great unwashed from a very privileged position (his whole misguided crew drains me of enthusiasm).

By default, it means he won't have much more of an idea about running the show than Muppet Gordon.

Long ago, I was told no one should hold any position of responsibility in a sawmill if they haven't first spent several years sweeping up and making t'tea. The observation came from an old old hand, and is absolutely transferable as wisdom to any sphere of human enterprise.

Instead, I understand that once more there are prospective MPs in both camps who've no experience of how the real world works, where the grist actually has to be ground. A good number of selected candidates are parachuted into safe seats because 'the party' wants them.

Oh? And how about the local electorate then? Do they want them? (I'll laugh like a drain if one or two of the really obvious cases lose their shirts.)

Anyway, I'm already fed up listening to it all, and wish candidates had to have a long proven track record in an honest profession. (This obviously excludes any media/PR/political researcher/trade union 'work'.) In fact, didn't you and I work out, long ago, that the raging desire to stand for Parliament should probably be a *disqualifying* characteristic?

I usually come back around to thinking what a good idea the hereditary peers were. No axes to grind, merely a responsibility thrust upon them. Instead, in the upper second house now we have this tacky echo of recent election success, where the right dodgy donation gets you a seat for life.

Grief, at least some of the old lot were in seats originally won at the point of a sword. You know where you stand with that, eh?

At home I'm still in the doghouse, having got Alison some flours for Valentines Day. (Yes, flours, as in self-raising and plain.) I thought it was a good gag, with the added bonus of useful by-product. For my troubles, I got a big helping of tongue pie. Huh, wimmin!

To try and pour oil on the matrimonial waters I did then whisk herself off for a romantic night out. This involved, as usual, a truckload of oak needing delivery. This time, it was up onto the Cotswolds.

After a moderately posh hotel room had been secured nearby, we dropped the beams in the customer's garden, beside the 'his and hers' Range Rover and Aston Martin in the drive… it was that kind of parish. However, when we trucked on back towards supper we realised that our footwear was somewhat soiled for the hotel in question. No worries, we'll wander up this lane, hop that gate, and wander down that footpath, wiping away the mud on the grass.

Sadly this plan went belly up when we discovered that there were a score and a half of two-year-old polo ponies out wintered on the field, and who'd been fed along the path. Mud everywhere. Still, we did get to meet some rather smart youngstock. (For those with such interests there were chestnuts and bays, each seemingly cast from one of two jelly moulds. I'd guess that there is techno-breeding assistance going on. I know artificial breeding techniques aren't allowed in racing circles, but I'd wager a quid they're in use thereabouts. As well as appearances, the chestnuts with blazes tend to grumpiness, but the bays were all just lovely. One very biddable chap promised he'd sit real still if I wanted to pop the padlock on the gate and give him a leg-up onto the flatbed. I declined, given that, in that particular vicinity, horse thievery is very likely an act of treason, carrying draconian penalties.)

To make ourselves presentable enough to get in the hotel door we had to dally at a roadside puddle, dodging traffic to hold one foot up at a time, scrubbing with a brush I had handy. Ha, romance lives.

And lastly, if you're sick of me, your moment is here.

Another filmmaker has been in touch (my peculiarities seem irresistible to them, but are then immediately countered by a singularly un-photogenic appearance).

Anyway, this lass knew how I'd hit it off last summer with a couple of Siberian Nenet birds who were over here singing about their reindeer (it's a long story). We'd had an immediate connection through our shared experience of livestock husbandry, and spent a happy evening trying to translate Siberian/Dartmoor vernacular terms for some of our more grubby livestock tasks. They were very gracious about the Galloway fillet I supplied for tea – especially as they had lodgings with a veggie couple locally, and weren't used to quite so many lentils.

Now yon filmmaker wants to ship me out onto the far tundra, and film the return visit. I'm game, but she's struggling to gather funds.

Alison is raising a collection, although she promises to stop when she hits the price of a one-way ticket.

Oksana and Tatyana *N. Shaw and C. Hillyer*

Spring 2010

Blue monkeys

As I'm sure you've long suspected, my farming operations are dictated by the latest developments in agri-technology. I can't get out in the morning, to see if the mummy cows are having their baby cows, if I haven't got to hand the latest report on up-to-date genetics. Filling the round feeders with bales needs input from this week's research on the methane these cows will burp at me. And as for spreading poop on the mowing ground, in the vague hope that it'll grow a crop of grass with which I can start the whole process all over again… Well obviously, I'll need some fangled GPS system to tell me which corner of the field needs that bit more. (In fact, fine-tuning our 'bovine waste recycling' is generally led by when and where the unbroken clump of muck suddenly breaks up or, conversely, when a handful of bale cord gets hooked into the spreader chains.)

Well, to be bang up to date with cutting-edge farm news… I've picked up my first Chinese lantern.

It was a lot of very flimsy paper, a couple of bent sticks, and yes, a nasty little piece of wire. Should such a thing fall into my mowing fields it could easily end up packed away in a bale of forage, with the piece of wire finally lodging in the guts of one of my cows. Now while I've some very moth-eaten old ladies, who don't raise as good a crop of calves as I might desire, I wouldn't wish this fate upon them.

I also have some cattle that are very special indeed – to me at least – and should that end befall them I would be apoplectic with rage. Happily, the chain of events would be spread over such a time as to leave me unaware of who exactly had done this to a beast, which is probably just as well. I suppose, should I happen upon some bozos lighting more such things at that moment, then my own fuse might get lit. (This really is not a spectacle you would wish to view from close up. Trust me.)

Let's be optimistic. We could view these things as some kind of involuntary swaling tool. Where we are only allowed, under our enviro schemes, to fire lawn-sized areas of overgrown rough… one of these lanterns might fire a large tract one day, leaving me with acres of blame-free fresh growth. (The local 'controlled burns' this spring have so far proved to be largely uncontrolled, requiring an average of five fire appliances to beat them into submission.)

Lastly, it does occur that the act of setting one, or 20, of these things must, by its nature, be an act of littering. I mean, unless you're going to chase across the countryside after them…?

A family outing saw us off to the flicks t'other day, for to watch sci-fi 3D spectacle *Avatar*. Wow, double wow! It is indeed visually as stunning as the hype, if somewhat lacking in other departments. The anorexic giant Smurfs gallivanting round the alien jungle tickled us mightily, although my party had to suppress a cheer as the mighty 'home-tree' came down (I was then busily rigging out and converting, in my mind).

The whole embarrassing gamut of clichéd toe-curlingly Americanised view of the world – albeit transferred to an imaginary other world – was a bit of a shame. The idea that interstellar mineral exploitation would be an 'American' operation, overseen by US marines, is just a touch parochial. That the loss of the Smurfs' land and culture parallels treatment of Native Americans is OK, as a cultural mirror, I suppose. Shame the real ones didn't get to chuck their oppressors back into the Atlantic though? Oh, hang on, that'd mean we'd still have the bozos here. Sorry Tonto, they're all yours old pal.

Alison speculates that the tree-falling sequence reflected the Twin Towers coming down in New York, with disbelief etched on the faces of the onlookers, as an iconic colossus was being razed by the 'baddies'. I'm sure it's all very Freudian.

I do recall reading a sci-fi short story, written long, long ago, about a physically disadvantaged man employed, as I remember, to telepathically control a tall vigorous bipedal alien doing useful work on some planet hostile to humankind. The alien was everything the operator wasn't, and sure enough the human soon discovered he didn't want to 'come back'. The story was called, if my memory serves, *Call me Joe*, or some such. (I did read this once, about 30 years ago, so forgive me if the edges are a bit fuzzy.) I wonder if Mr Cameron read the same book?

Mind you, I was also wondering if a Ms Rowling had read how Douglas Adams' engagingly dishevelled detective Dirk Gently had stepped into another realm, by walking, a bit sidling like, through a London railway station?

I'd better stop here, before I upset anyone else with better legal funds than me.

Anyway, what a remarkable and enjoyable bit of escapism *Avatar* is. I doff my weather-worn hat to all concerned.

'Show-and-tell' with the Coaker urchins

There is a bitter irony in my life just now. We have had to jab several big weaned heifer calves, thought to have cycled a bit quicker than I was expecting and 'stolen' the bull, to rid them of unwanted surprises next summer. Backalong, Joe also spotted – in time – a freshly calved pedigree Angus heifer get herself tangled up with the wrong bull within very few days of her calving. Another jab.

Conversely, there's a Riggit Galloway I can't get to hold to the bull, any bull, for love or money. She is one of the two 'Floras' I managed to secure from one of the Riggit herds – Mochrum – restarted in the eighties.

The heifers were both *in utero* when Scottish breeder Miss Flora Stewart sadly passed away. The estate wasn't that interested in the more arcane lines that Miss Flora had bred★, and quickly dispersed most of them, including the Riggits. These two were born the following year, and left skidding about with some store cattle, before good fortune found them heading

One of the 'Floras'

south. They are, for me, the last drop of an irreplaceable vintage, and frankly I'd have crawled over broken glass to obtain them.

For them to now be living on the hill with an unrelated Riggit bull would have, I hope – given what could so easily have happened – delighted Miss Flora.

Anyway, the best-looking one cycles as regular as you like, and has now had her chance of various husbands, but conceives not. T'vet has tried various techno tweaks, but to no avail. The heifer blooms in every other way, getting steadily plumper, and we're now wandering if we should shut her in with nowt but straw to get some flesh off her again.

We'll see.

Flora had breeding groups of the three different coloured Belted Galloways: Whites with both black points and red, the aforementioned Riggits, and, rarest of all, a beautiful herd of solid red Galloways. (I say 'a herd'; I mean 'the herd'.)

She was by every account a most remarkable character, and simply a lovely person. I kick myself over and over for never getting to meet her, beyond passing pleasantries in the pens at Castle Douglas.

I suspect that the poor teachers who have to deal with my kids dread the little urchins' arrival. Daddy kindly sends them ready charged with difficult questions, and scurrilously supplies science info of all the wrong kind.

The poor lady vicar who comes in to skool once a week and tries to spread the good word gets asked for proof that would hold up in court. Agnes, when she was at primary, was especially proficient at this, and would read up on other religions to spice up the discussion. Eventually we decided it was probably kinder to show some pity. The lessons were treated as an extension of care in the community.

For the record, I object strongly to my offspring being told, as facts, stories that are demonstrably not actually verifiable. You believe whatever you wish, but don't foist it onto my kids.

RE classes notwithstanding, I also notice a bit of a bunny-hugger veggie liberal trend among the teachers generally. I wonder how they reacted last week, when John and Polly went to skool jumping up and down with excitement cos Daddy had finally nailed the squirrel that was coming to the bird table (Daddy had hung out of the bedroom window, at dawn, with the musket to achieve this). It was all we could do to stop them taking it in as a 'show-and-tell' trophy.

Bluegrass sacrilege!

For my birthday treat my adorable little wife took me out on the razz. Backalong I'd been listening to Hayseed Dixie, a pretty daft bluegrass-cum-rock cover band (I know, it sounds ridiculous, but it works. Trust me on this). Well they were noticed to be playing locally, and we just had to go along and check it out.

Arriving on stage already clutching bottles of beer, sporting a selection of beards and bib-and-brace overalls, these ol' Southern boys set to with their geetars, banjos, fiddles and a mandolin, and charged into a selection of bluegrass takes on rock classics of my youth. Not surprisingly, AC/DC tunes feature heavily in their repertoire. It is all done with a degree of tongue-in-cheek humour (well, you could hardly keep a straight face could you?). If you're still struggling with the idea, imagine the illegitimate issue of a liaison between Oh Brother where art thou? and Spinal Tap.

Along the way they embrace the clichéd image of hill-billy backwoods America, both in song and banter. Lots of reference to moonshining and corn liquor. Introducing their song about alien abduction, they ask why abductees always claim to have had similarly… er… intrusive examinations? They close their set with a take on the 'duelling banjos' tune featured, you'll recall, in the fine instructional hawg husbandry movie Deliverance. Knowing this tune was likely in the set, I wore the T-shirt my cousin had sent specially. It sports the question 'If it's the "tourist season", why cain't we shoot 'em?'

The Hayseed Dixies are a raucous, funny night out, with lots of thigh-slapping yee-hawing if you're prepared to let your hair down. (It should be observed that some of those assembled appeared to be bluegrass 'enthusiasts', who were a bit nonplussed by it all. Poor souls.)

Some of us, however, got the joke from the first moment, and loved every minute of it. I'm sorry to admit that your humble scribe was impelled to get fuelled up, having discovered that some dang fool was only charging £2.30 for a double (sadly no single malts were on display, but a bottle of Jamesons was spied on the shelf). He subsequently jumped up and down a lot and, to the lasting embarrassment of his chauffeur and PA, sang-along at the top of his voice. She finally had to lead him away, like a balloon on a string.

Yee-ha! Don't miss the opportunity if it comes your way is my advice (and is, of course, my standard 'one size fits all' bit of advice).

Another birthday treat went past recently as well. The boy had been promised, once the mercury got above freezing, he could take some of his chums fishing. Well, the time soon came around, and off we went. To be sure they actually came home with something, this meant turning up at the trout farm with six 'enthusiastic' little hoodlums. For the first hour they did nothing but run up and down the bank shouting, and then get their lines tangled. No fish. After this hour, I gathered them round and laid down the law. Be quiet, or there will be no fish. That worked like a charm. The minute the fish started to move it was all the bloodthirsty little monsters could do to keep pulling them out and clubbing them half to bits, and baiting hooks again. (The quietest, best-behaved of this gang, Dougie, was in charge of the net, and a priest. Jeez! Different boy once his blood's up!) It was, as they say, like shooting fish in a barrel.

Anyway, they loved it, and Dad had a good old time to boot. The only problem? Well the catch is that you pay by the kilo on your departure, and the fat little trout weighed a lot heavier than the wild little things the boy catches up here!

I won't go into the SFP mess. We're still lacking maps, and the RPA are making plausible promises that I don't quite believe.

Better crack on, lambing and calving apace.

After the watershed

It's been a pretty bruising winter on the hills. I haven't seen stock so needing the attentions of 'Dr Green' for some years.

The outdoor lying youngstock, both maiden heifers and first calvers, haven't enjoyed it much, and neither have the Cheviot ewes come to that. Conversely, the Scotch ewes looked pretty good as they came off the hill to lamb, and the older cows – both South Devons and Galloways – are mostly glossy and round. Beats me. As calving and lambing progress the effects of a late spring, following a long winter, will be revealed.

I didn't catch the 'lambing-live' telly show, or whatever it was called. (Oddly enough, I wasn't that interested, not fancying Ms

Humble, and having a surfeit of my own ovine headaches.) I understand there was much angst when anything went wrong.

Ha! I wonder how a show would've gone shot on some hillside in Scotland three weeks back, as March crashed into April? I believe it was pretty diabolic for anyone lambing just then, and have heard discreet reports of serious losses.

My favourite report, though, ends better. A 'mature' lady farmer of my acquaint calves a herd of Belts and Riggits on her tod, on a Dumfries hill. At 1am, the night it came in bad again that week, she heard a cow bawling. She went out into the gale, torch in hand, to find a cow had calved beside the feeder, and the calf was in the porridge. Now my friend is a game old stick, but couldn't move the calf and had to leave the outfit there until daylight. Sure enough, dawn found her trying to pull a stone-cold shivering calf out of the mud, in appalling conditions. The calf's nose was only just above the surface, and it came within an ace of drowning. My friend couldn't budge it, and then become stuck herself (trying to be diplomatic, she is 'quite mature', and of diminutive stature).

She had to abandon her wellies, and retreat in her socks. Once back to the house, she requisitioned the two lads who were due to do some work in the garden that day, and they set off with a wheelbarrow to recover the calf. Finally, with it in a byre, they got some colostrum out of the cow – Galloways aren't nearly as shirty as people would have you believe. Two days later, I hear, the calf was galloping around the hillside, and the wellies were recovered.

Anyway, not all the stories coming out of Scotland this spring (or Dartmoor come to that) have such happy endings. It has been a long winter, and up here it ain't over yet.

Back to the niceties of what we can (or, more pointedly, cannot) see of farm stock on TV. You'll notice when it goes 'wrong': they're a bit coy about the whole issue. Some deal with it, some don't, lest it offends, but there is generally a lot of tippy-toeing about. There is a pretty big irony in the whole attitude given that after the watershed you can watch the most grisly of films, while ads for computer games encouraging the kids to shoot/stab/disembowel virtual baddies are run at skool home time. Of course, you might try to keep the kids away from TV nastiness by sending 'em off to bed at 9pm. Unfortunately they might then access the Internet from their computers, or even their mobile phones. Believe me, what they can be looking at therein would curdle your cocoa!

Funny old world isn't it?

For the record, my three rug-rats still don't yet have mobile phones, or computers/tellies in their rooms. Conversely, they know very well what might happen to a lamb born out in the sleet, or where the bucket calf from two years ago just went. (Bless their hearts, although the kids loved him dearly, they didn't bat an eyelid when they realised he was being loaded. I think John went out to say goodbye as I dug out the paperwork, but that was as far as it went.)

I'm not sure what it says of me, as a parent, but I regard it as very reassuring.

Now then, have you noticed that all the news reports on the Icelandic volcano have been blathering about the disruption to air traffic? There have been a few gags comparing the banking collapse, even the cod wars, but there's something else you ought to know.

The last time this particular volcano went bang, in 1821, it erupted on and off for 18 months. Now I haven't got much info on the implications of the current eruption, but if it goes on like this for 18 months I suspect that the travel interruption will be about the last of your worries, unless you're trying to flee the Northern Hemisphere. Sadly, surfing the web for historical weather info and dendrological records soon runs into disputed material, caught up in the global warming row. I'll try and find you out some more d'rectly.

It is worth noting that another Icelandic volcano – Laki – erupted in 1783, spewing a toxic cloud across much of Europe and North America, which poisoned tens of thousands and fried all manner of crops (with sulphur dioxide and hydrogen fluoride). Really, it did. Back in Iceland, it killed half the livestock, and a quarter of the human population.

This volcano is different to Laki, but…

Meantime, if you want an upside… Wouldn't this be a good time for the whinging cabin crew to have their wretched strike?

The light at the end of the tunnel

We were TB testing in that nasty cold Easter sleet, in a howling gale (thankfully while the precipitation was full of lumps, the cattle weren't). It was that cold that poor veterinary could hardly reload the jabbing gear.

To keep the paperwork dry, Alison had to shelter in a handily parked Land Rover cab. (Somehow, building a race indoors to test Galloways just doesn't seem right does it? One day I'll get round to doing something about some shelter, but then 'one day' we'll all do a lot of stuff, won't we boys and girls.)

While the lads fed cattle down the chute to the vet I worked the gate, read tags and relayed – or rather, hollered – numbers and skin readings to our clerk. To save some of the shouting, and 'What was that?'-ing, I'd hold up the requisite number of fingers to indicate skin readings. (An 8mm skin reading would, obviously enough, be eight fingers held aloft, nine for 9mm etc.) Alison would squint through the sleet-splattered windscreen, trying to keep it all tickety-boo. This worked OK until the vet measured an 11. He sympathetically realised my predicament, as I looked perplexed. I had to mumble my admission with some embarrassment that I would struggle, given the weather conditions, to do better than a ten and a half.

He didn't think he could do better, for similar reasons, and anyway, we considered Alison might get altogether the wrong idea. We shouted out readings above 10mm.

Strangely enough, later in the week, after we'd finished doing the readings in similar conditions, we weren't in the mood to do the bit of dehorning/deknackering I generally aim to tidy up just then. It could wait til kinder weather.

While it hadn't been especially late for spring to get going up here, I believe that off the moor there were grumblings about the lateness of the season. This manifested itself to me as a greatly shortened supply of fodder on the market. I was buying a bit steadily, having kept back a bit of my own supply in reserve. Then suddenly, as the cold dry March waved 'bye bye', and April arrived with snow and miserable northerlies, the available supplies dried up markedly. With less than a fortnight's grub on the place, and a month's worth of feeding to do, I really had the willies for a day or two. Luckily Cameron phoned back with a price on some haylage which, while I didn't like the figures, I was very glad to hear he'd secured. The situation eased again a week later, but it was a bit scary for a minute.

The persistent cold sleet has also had a detrimental effect on some of the stock. The mature cows look just fine and dandy, shrugging off the weather and licking themselves. Less happy with the late spring were some of the outwintered youngstock, and the in-bye ewes. A soaking summer, several rough patches through the winter proper, and now a cold spring, has knocked 'em about a bit.

My boy, stockman Joe and I went off backalong to recover a Galloway steer that wasn't looking too chipper from a bleak windswept newtake. The bullock didn't want his sweeties that morning – very unusual – and was breathing very shallow. Time he had some antibotics and was out of the weather for a day or two. Walking him down to the trailer the wretched beast kept diving into the gorse to sulk. I spent a happy 30 minutes following him through deep clumps, while my assistants kindly shouted directions and words of encouragement from the peripheries.

Once loaded a bit of TLC sorted the steer out without any long-term damage, although I was nicely porcupined with gorse prickles for a day or two. Lovely.

And now spring has made a guest appearance. To be seasonal, with fancies turning light, my lovely wife and I have been dancing round the breakfast table (B52s' 'Loveshack' on the wireless, since you ask). Youngest offspring Polly was disgusted. She loudly announced 'You used to do that, then you had us, and got old.' Hmm, thanks Polly.

To be fair though, having spent many, many hours trudging up and down dale catching lambs and calves to apply some rings and tags and stuff, I have to admit she may well have a point. (Alison, obviously, is only 27, and will firmly be remaining so.) My knees feel like they need a couple of strokes of the grease gun, and my feet are generally pretty hurty by evening. I would tell you about the whiff radiating from my leather boots, but I appreciate that you might very well be reading this over a spot of tiffin, so I'll refrain. My back aches, and I'm perpetually soaked in a heady cocktail including varying ratios of iodine, amniotic fluid, diesel, lamb poop and the like. (Oops, sorry – I wasn't going to go there, was I?)

To close, here some maxims that came through on an email this morning.

1. Light travels faster than sound. This is why some people appear bright until you hear them speak.

2. Change is inevitable, except from a vending machine.
3. Those who live by the sword get shot by those who don't.
4. Nothing is foolproof to a sufficiently talented fool.
5. The things that come to those who wait will be the scraggly junk left by those who got there first.
6. The shin bone is a device for finding furniture in a dark room.
7. A fine is a tax for doing wrong. A tax is a fine for doing well.
8. When you go into court you are putting yourself into the hands of 12 people who weren't smart enough to get out of jury duty.
9. The light at the end of the tunnel is probably a train coming.

One-handed chainsaws and tagging calves

I've been reading about various visits, by dignitaries, to the great unwashed (mostly blatantly looking for a vote or two, thanks awfully). The Minister of such and such has been shaking hands over yonder, while the Shadow Minister for so and so has been kissing babies down along lee. Strangely though, you haven't read about any ministerial visits around here.

I suppose this may be because, evidently, my reputation goes far enough. You see, when some canvassing politician's ankle wound has started to fester, gangrene set in, and an amputation become likely, I will try my hardest to convince a judge that 'Seize 'em Gyp' is the vernacular command used to try and get the collie to sit holding his paw up. Reps and religious salesmen are seldom seen either (or at least, are never seen again).

Over the weekend the moor has been alive with kids hiking, with Ten Tors practice and various Duke of Edinburgh award groups out and about. We have to spend a fair deal of time going round closing gates behind the few less responsible kids. (Such allegations will no doubt be strenuously denied; perhaps it's the weekend pixies.)

Anyroad, being bang up to date with things, I've also been wrestling calves on the hill, getting tags in their lugholes, and rubber rings on unwanted appendages. This morning, as I grabbed a strapping Angus baby – which big hairy 'Fiona' had hidden in the gorse for several days, so it damn well took some grabbing – a group of said kids hiked past on a bridlepath, about 30 yards away. The moment her calf squawked Fiona came bellowing over, in the manner one becomes accustomed to, and circled me eye to eye. As I did what I needed to do she was roaring her head off at me. I alternately smacked her with the long-handled crook and jabbed her on the nose with the ring pliers to keep her at bay. And here's the thing. As far as I could tell, the kids – who could hardly have failed to clock this bloke being attacked by a wild cow – completely ignored the spectacle. They didn't appear to slow, stop to gawp, or even run on quicker. They just kept plodding, heads down. In their position I think I'd have stopped to watch; possibly I'd have pulled up a rock to have a sandwich and enjoy the show, maybe have a flutter with my fellow hikers on the result... perhaps I'm interested in different things to hiking yoof.

I was intrigued by an ad in a well-known farming glossy last week. The ad was for a market-leading chainsaw/brushcutter manufacturer, and featured a suitably rugged-looking chap, looking purposefully into the middle distance – I expect he is called Bruce, or possibly Brad – and one of this firm's chainsaws. All well and good so far. The readership would very likely be the kind of folk who'd be needing a chainsaw to massacre overgrown hedges, shape the point on a fencing strut, or just bang up some firewood for the house. And the model featured? I notice it was the top-handled model, carefully balanced so it can be used one handed, and which is very carefully only sold to trained tree surgeons. Tell certain farmers of our acquaint they can buy a chainsaw that can be operated with one hand, and they'll immediately start wandering what multi-tasking jobs they could incorporate with banging up some firewood. One-handed fag rolling perhaps, or just a bit of idle nose picking. In fact, on cold days, wouldn't it be nice to be able to keep one hand in your pocket!

Larch pox in the spring

I made a classic hill farmer mistake yesterday. I went out in the Land Rover to a couple of site meetings off the moor. My jaunt took me to Exeter, and on up through Crediton. I saw lush acres of growing grass, stocked with glossy contented stock. Arable crops were up and doing, and even some silage cut. At the end of the day I returned to Cold Comfort Farm on

Dartmoor, where the ground was picked bare and yellowing, and my dispirited Scotch ewes were sitting around watching for something – anything – to show its head above the turf. The cows were stood lowing at the feeders, wondering if someone would find them some more fodder, and the Dartmoor mares were carefully picking the tips off the gorse bushes. (I've noticed the Scotch ewes have a great fondness for the fragrant flowers of the common, or 'European' gorse – that's the taller one that flowers in the spring – while the shorter 'Western' variety gives September some colour.)

It's never easy coming home from lowland outings at this time of year, but 2010 looks like being a vintage year in that respect. The stock has been spread over much greater areas than normal through calving and lambing, to try and 'find a pick'. Certainly they're spread thinner than my knees would prefer, as I've tramped miles trying to see everything mornings. The main mob of Galloways are now turned out the gate onto the common. That must be a big enough area to find a pick, surely.

My outing yesterday had included measuring and valuing a fallen oak log. I seldom consider single logs, but this 'un was over 4 feet in diameter, over the 22 feet of the first length. Some of the material therein is of a pretty high grade, but with 10 tonnes of it in one length, lying down over a 45-degree bank, the logistics remain an issue. Poor unfortunate Chris (who hauls my bigger logs) has been warned, and has gone away shaking his head, muttering darkly. I think he was threatening to emigrate.

Speaking of emigrating, the threat of warmer weather has drawn the drystone walling fairies from their winter quarters, creaking and groaning, and pre-booking dates with the osteopath. I notice one team is a man down this season. Ben has, I'm told, gone to New Zealand. 'That's a bit much,' I ventured, 'he only had to say he didn't fancy it this year.'

The news has come through recently that 'sudden oak death' has mutated and crept into a few larch plantations, which have had to be hurriedly felled to prevent spores spreading.

While this is of some concern to me, it was also somewhat worrying to the powers that be, in forestry, so they hopped in a helicopter recently and upped their search area.

'Oh bother!' said they (actually, I believe it was a bit stronger than 'bother'). The search has revealed more. Now the needles are out, and the spores are blowing, there is a certain amount of panic abroad. While the helicopter safely got back to *terra firma*, the industry is fast heading into a tailspin.

One site, which I won't name, has some hundreds of acres suspected infected, or in immediate danger. Tests are still in the lab, but if confirmed it's likely to be felled with immediate effect. Not selectively thinned on an ongoing basis you understand, with small coupes clear-felled on a planned rotation: the whole lot knocked over in one hit. To put it in some kind of perspective, the logs on this one site would, if crosscut to 12 feet and stacked in a single row 2 metres high, make a pile something like 5 kilometres long!

The timber is to be stockpiled initially until it is clarified whether the spores might be carried on the wagons. Current thinking is that the logs could possibly be peeled on site, and then carted to a sawmill, with the loads being disinfected as they go. The jury is still out on this, as boffins scratch their noggins.

I haven't heard yet, but I assume the aim will be to limit the outbreak to as small an area as possible. Certainly, no one will want it to get out of the Westcountry, although how long before spores float across the Bristol Channel is anybody's guess. How the industry will cope with the ongoing logistics of this operation is equally open speculation.

I've heard no more yet regarding native oaks, beyond that sessile oak can become infected, but only if growing in close proximity to the said larch. We'll keep our fingers crossed on that shall we?

Meanwhile though, adding gravity to a serious business, it is now suspected that other commercial conifers, most notably our mainstay, Douglas fir, are also susceptible to the newly mutated fungus. Being the benchmark species for quality lowland UK softwood production, this will up the stakes in a very big way. You will be hearing a lot more on this.

Right. Onwards. I do hope we'll see you all at the Devon County Show, where our good friend Alison Bunning is exhibiting a lovely little Riggit Galloway heifer that originated up here. My wife Alison is also planning to attend, giving moral support.

This is, we think, the first time in a century or more that such a beast has appeared in the public arena. Do drop by and admire her. Perhaps, if you speak softly, and proffer a hank of sweet hay, you might be permitted to scratch her behind the ear, or even run your hand down her back. (I want to be very clear about this. I am talking about the heifer.)

Eating off a roof slate

Acting on advice, I've taken a holiday. The cows have nearly stopped calving – which isn't the same as saying they have all calved… oh no Siree, not by a long chalk I'm afraid – and the sheep are mostly out of the mowing ground. Joe is busy spreading the remaining poop, and might get to smear some molehills about d'rectly. So it all begins again!

Anyway… a bit of a break. To be honest our holiday features, once again, the wife and I taking the lorry off delivering timber. It was another load to the smart garden job up on the Cotswolds, so another night out in a posh hotel was called for. Hang the expense.

The run up was lovely. Blazing sun, M5 half empty – I don't know how come by, but hey! You takes yer luck where you finds it. As we trundled along across the Somerset Levels, the hawthorn blossom was right on the button for miles. Passing Brent Knoll on the left, looking right, south and east, the hedges merged into a sea of creamy white. Outstanding. The only fly in this ointment came when we pulled in to the services for an industrial-strength coffee, and discovered the coffee machine knackered. Argh! Alison and I are both fond of a good coffee, so we were soon chewing our nails, missing our fix. As traffic thickened past Bristol, tempers frayed a touch.

Luckily though, we were soon off the motorway, up at the delivery address and off-loaded, headed for our hotel.

It was the kind of place with mullioned stone windows, oak floors and significant yew trees dotted around the grounds. I don't begrudge my little wife these luxuries from time to time (goodness knows she deserves it, floundering in my chaotic wake). But I do struggle so with the proper form in such environs. My hick background always leads to some inappropriate behaviour or other. There's often a shiny receptionist/waiter, smiling obsequiousness, but radiating loud and clear behind their eyes that I'm out of my depth, and only allowed in on sufferance (I care not one jot, happily, and generally trample straight on).

I had remembered my shoes this time, and didn't need to scrub my boots in a roadside puddle, or partake of an evening meal in my stockinged feet. I'd even hidden the lorry round the back for fear of upsetting the more refined residents.

No, this time it was my continued inability to get the hang of how the other half dine that let me down. We'd shared drinkies out in the grounds with a local cattle-breeding pal, watching the sun sink and the world go past, and all was well. Then he pushed off, as Alison and I repaired to the lounge to peruse the menu for our blow-out tea.

Now I do make an effort, really I do, but we were offered a selection of courses in foreign languages, silly portions, and mixtures of palettes that might've been designed to dazzle but in reality, just confuse and annoy. The pompous mixture of French and Italian words in the menu struck me as a bit ironic, given that the delightful and attentive staff were drawn from local Gloucester stock, alongside a couple of very sweet girls from, I believe, Slovakia. I grumbled.

Eventually we made our choices, went through, and Alison started to speak to me again. (She was quite cross, having made me promise not to make a scene this time.)

As a bottle of pink wine softened my edges a bit – I'd fancied a nice fruity sounding Kiwi plonk, but herself pointed out that it was £45 a go, so that was out – a raging appetite took hold, and I dug in. The pea mousse and asparagus spear starter was interesting – but funnily enough, called something else altogether, and the Welsh mountain lamb main course delightful. I did gently prod to find out how the Welsh had managed to rear mountain lamb to slaughter by the last week in May, but 'Magda' couldn't quite find the right English phrases (Alison was mouthing 'from the freezer' behind her hand). Anyway, apart from the side dish of force-fed goose innards it was very nice, and I'd certainly travel to have young Magda fussing over me so.

The best bit, however, was the crockery. At least two of my courses arrived on reclaimed roofing slates. Complete with nail holes. Really, really, really: as sure as I am sitting here telling you, I've discovered that the great and the good not only pay hard coin of the realm to eat silly little portions, with daft made-up names, they'll even eat it off old roofing slates. Absolutely blinking fascinating to a peasant like me.

And here's the thing. I've realised you and I could think up some even more exotic menus. We're going to make a packet. Obviously there's some soup dish we could work on involving various bovine amniotic and placental substances we have in abundance, seasonally. Garnish might well be a cheeky little rye grass 'pickled salad, *à la clamp*'. It'll be best if it's shot through with blue mould, like that green cheese. To follow, I suspect, there's a rather attractive smelling 'recycled ovine colostrum' pudding to be found. (And don't try and tell me you've never noticed.)

I realise now that more outlandish it sounds, and the more we charge for it, the happier they'll be. Look, I'll put it in some kind of order, while you see if you can rustle up a TV celebrity chef to run with it.

Basket weaving

One of my allotted tasks during spring is to count the stock on my 'patch' of common. This is an enjoyable, if energetic, job for an old bloke, involving trudging several miles up one river catchment, crossing the head of another, on up over a 1700-foot brow, then a similar distance back down a third valley, zigzagging along to try and look in all the crannies along the way. (Yes yes, I could do it on a quad. I still prefer Shanks's pony.) I have to go sometime in May, although I leave it til late in the month or I find it a bit lonely up there.

Well this time, despite leaving in fine weather with a good forecast, it was soon lashing down through thick fog, and blowing a gale.

I should've smelled a rat when I'd counted almost all of my own cows about 20 yards outside the moor gate. They obviously knew what was coming. By noon there I was, sat with my back to a hilltop stone cross chewing on a sandwich, thinking it would lift in a minute (forecast had admitted there might've been the odd light shower somewhere through the day). Did it lift? Did it buggery. When I set off again, bored with watching fog billow past and dampness seep down the cross, I was generally navigating by wind direction, only catching fleeting glimpses of odd groups of black bullocks lower down, as the curtains would momentarily lift. I bumped into two groups of kids out hiking, head down following the compass… mmm fun!

I eventually found most of what I was still looking for, and I could wobble homewards satisfied. Curiously, as I dropped off the last ridge, the rain stopped, and the sun came out. Hmm, that'll be a three-hour 'light shower' will it?

Even better, as Alison and I socialised with some farming pals 20 miles away that night (the Malseeds' combined wedding anniversary and various birthday celebrations), I ascertained the location of the group I was missing. Result! Anyroad, let's hope the Met Office buck up their act by the time I've got grass to cut.

The two smallest Coaker pups have been sent home with a permission slip from skool – for they must seek our permission to do just about anything. This time, the kids are off on a day out learning about traditional, sustainable local skills. Hmm, says the wife and I. And what are traditional local skills? Dartmoor pony-branding classes? Wrestling Galloway bull calves to the ground to tag and castrate them? Are the kids going to be taught how to dog Scotch ewes out of difficult ghoyles? Perhaps it'll be lessons in clamping teddies or swedes, how to make a decent larch gate, or that modern hybrid skill, drystone walling from the digger seat.

Certainly I'd like my kids to know how to safely use a chainsaw, and tow a trailer – skills which now must involve formal training – and how to select thrifty tups and docile, easy calving bulls (something for which they'll probably not find formal training).

No. What they're actually going to be taught is willow weaving.* And could they bring a packed lunch with as little wrapping as possible, to help explain sustainability.

Now funnily enough, the class includes several tackers from tribes which have been skidding about Dartmoor for some centuries, probably longer. They would, within close family, be able to pick up many of the skills you and I might value.

Meanwhile, their cultural connection, and the social bonds and currents within, often remain quite invisible to the degree-holding settlers, including those taking the skool register. I suspect some snatch a tantalising glimpse, and there are a few who assimilate quite quickly and very soon could've been here forever. (I want to be clear about this. We're not trying to hold back the tide, and generally embrace incomers at various levels. But some of us aren't blind to our cultural heritage either, and won't have it walked over.)

Having said all this, on consultation with one of my cultural gurus, a certain Mr Pearse, I'm assured that willow weaving would very much have been a traditional skill. In fact, he went on to describe an old picture he was looking at, showing a huge withy basket full of about 50 (sustainably) dead rabbits.

I said, 'Should I climb down off my high horse, Colin?' 'No, Anton,' he said, 'you get right back aboard.'

And now I'm off to raise a glass to Dennis Hopper. After a spectacularly mercurial movie-acting (and directing) career – and a lifestyle hardly conducive to a long life – he somehow survived to a respectable vintage before cashing in his chips. While his genial rambling and mumbling performances on film could only endear him to anyone who recognised his 'confused' state, his life off screen was no less confused (he was once reported in his local paper as having had a spill on his motorbike whilst 'feeling no pain'). He could then belie his amiable burnt-out hippy persona, and deliver subtle, dark and sinister performances, quietly notching up a notable catalogue of work.

None the less, it's the dishevelled affable 'Easy Riding' character I'll remember, and to whom we'll raise a dram.

Dialects and electronic tags

I expect many of you have your own tales of frustration with the ongoing lack of paperwork to fill out the SFP. Lack of forms, lack of remapped maps, lack of will to do any more paperwork at a very busy time of year.

Our household is, at time of typing, rueing the continuing lack of maps, which then seriously affects our ability to safely make a SFP claim. The clock is ticking ominously. Alison had, when I got back in the house t'other night, to top her afternoon coffee mug up with a generous slosh of Stag's Breath single malt. We both recognise that this isn't going to get the forms filled in, but I was sympathetic.

I seem to recall the big RPA boss promised faithfully that all the new maps would be on farm by the end of April. It would appear he wasn't being absolutely truthful in this statement, and that his pants may very well be on fire.

Wouldn't it be nice if the man who promised us the paperwork in time for his own deadline now faced the same penalties that we do?

🦋

Ah! Now, these 'ere electronic ear tags fer to stick in the yows, or yaws as we call them in the Westcountry. (I will have to write a piece on these nuances of farming dialect one day. The origins of some terms are deeper than you're expecting, and very interesting if you're of that bent.)

Anyway, it occurs to me, how long before some enterprising shepherd starts peeling away the plastic so he can insert the chips under the skin of his breeding ewes? When a mob then disappear off the hill – for such thievery is rife in some parts – he might then let it be known that they have gone, and advise that there's cash rewards for information leading to the identification of the perpetrator.

The chip is, as I understand, a positive individual ID, and once hidden under the skin it would likely be very hard for a 'tea leaf' to find and remove – unlike the stupid tag of course. Run through the scanner at a market or abattoir though, it could still be read – in fact, wouldn't it be obvious something was up, as the tea leaf would've put his own tag in, so a scanner would pick up two readings on one sheep?

And now there would then be a financial paper trail back to a very worried man indeed, for you and I both know some hill farmers take a very grave view of such thievery. Some of them are wont to overreact (at least one of us might very well be such a man even).

Now your humble diarist must condemn such improper use of the chips, and whatever sanctions such a flock owner might impose. Nonetheless, we're watching with interest.

🦋

Sorry, back to the niceties of dialect. I love the variety of dialect and communities still hidden in the UK's backwoods. There are millennia of heritage visible just beneath the veneer of wealthy blow-ins and urban migrants. Deep amongst the Welsh hills you'll find families that have been farming those slopes since, well, since at least before the Romans I would guess. Across the Downlands in the south there are some extraordinarily deep-rooted folk. (Wasn't it in Wilts or Dorset that some ancient DNA recovered from an archaeological site was matched almost exactly – improbably exactly even – to a local bloke, propping up the public bar just down the road, clutching a mug of cider and wondering what all the fuss was about?)

Out on the Scottish isles the last millennia of seaborne movements are still etched clearly across the population and their dialect. Even amongst urban Scotland's abrasive drawl there is a distinct linguistic trail tiptoeing across a thousand years and a sea crossing.

Vernacular Cornish farming terms have a clear affinity with those across the Irish Sea, although the terms have been assimilated into an Anglo-Saxon tongue.

It's a precious thing, and all the more so since it's almost invisible to urban British academia. It continues quite happily to evolve organically, as all things must.

With this in mind I was intrigued by a report a week or two back from some worthy body desperately concerned about racism in rural communities. Apparently, having a lack of ethnic diversity in our communities makes us all terribly racist. Oh! said I, and where exactly are the BNP councillors all voted into office? In the event of parliamentary fudge leading to proportional representation, which communities are going to be responsible for the first BNP MPs?

Is it in these leafy bucolic beds of rural fascism, where the 'white only' population must surely be driving 'ethnic' newcomers out with pitchforks? Strangely no, it isn't. This is a truth too big for the body doing the study to admit, and does in fact lead to some very disturbing and fundamental questions about multiculturalism and diversity in communities.

Anyway, I find their conclusions regarding rural Britain not a little insulting, on several levels.

Summer 2010

Extracts from *The Orcadian Whelk Harvesters Digest*

One of the problems with writing a diary for publication is my failing memory. I can't for the life of me recall what I wrote last year, or the year before that. I can't exactly pinpoint whether or not I've had published the tale of Maurice Clapton's slurry lagoon and the parachutist, or the sorry outcome of the Heckling twins' attempt to stage a 'Middle White gilt most like its owner' beauty contest. I might've, I might not have. Damned if I can recall. (Should an actual Maurice Clapton or Heckling twin turn up for a royalty cheque they'll be disappointed, seeing as those I refer to are firmly fictitious. However, I will certainly try and winkle a story or two out of them, to be sure.)

And writing for several publications as I do makes things even more complicated. (Oh, you didn't realise? Well don't let it upset you; it's you I really love. The others mean nothing to me, I promise.)

As a matter of principle I try and make each piece different, even if Alison has scurrilously suggested that I just send the same piece to each of the three editors with this Monday's editorial deadline (tempting as this idea is, seeing as the readership can hardly be overlapping twixt *British Farmer and Grower, The Digest of the Orcadian Whelk Harvesters Co-operative* or *The United Piano-tuners Gazette*).

Anyway, where we're really heading with this is to apologise if I start repeating myself.

It's hard to tell you that I've been spending long days in a tractor cab chasing rows of grass without it sounding just like any other diary entry at this time of year, or possibly your own diary. I could wax lyrical on the relative merits of diesel as a skin cream, or the misery of dust-choked eyes, but I'm sure we've oft journeyed there before.

Well, it's still the same as ever. If I had an observation I could say it's all a little more tiresome, as I seem to seize up easier after a long day than I once did. Coming in of an evening admitting I'm a bit stiff doesn't have quite the same response as it used to, when uz was younger.

Thinking about it, I remember guffawing at a colleague who was greatly enamoured of a tractor he borrowed from

Rowing up hay in the latest hi-tech tractor

a neighbour because it had some fangled auto-mechanism or other. 'What on earth is the matter with you?' I asked, 'it's just more to go wrong.' 'No mate,' he responded, 'you don't understand. My knee creaks so much now that it's a dream just to hit a couple of buttons on the headlands, rather than have to arse around with clutches and brakes and widgets.'

Well, I'm ashamed to admit – although I roundly chastised him at the time for going soft – as the years go on I suspect I shall be sampling another slice of humble pie d'rectly (I'm already a bit whingy about the bust radio and the air-con on the tractor that's hooked to the baler).

Luckily, admitting I was horribly wrong regarding pretty much anything I've said previously is my default position. It's safer that way.

Onwards. To make a change from fretting over livestock plagues, we're currently watching the pox that is whistling through the Westcountry's larch plantations just now. It appears to be a mutation of the 'sudden oak death' fungus which has been grumbling around Devon and Cornwall's rhododendron population for a couple of years, and is now off through commercial larch woodland like a dose of salts. It doesn't easily move by other means, but as the needles come out in spring, spores erupt all over, wafting off like a windborne scalded cat

The official answer to this – and given the high mortality rate, there is a pretty big problem – is to clear-fell any plantation so affected. Details of how the timber can be moved and traded are still sketchy, but enquiries suggest that the spores don't easily move on felled logs, so some basic disinfection/hygiene protocols might be enough.

Unsurprisingly, government departments have been deafeningly quiet about all this. While they are following up aerial surveys, issuing felling orders, and controlling – after a fashion – the movement of felled material, they have manifestly forgotten to contact the quite limited number of businesses involved as a whole.

Most of us felling, hauling or processing local timber, have only heard about it anecdotally. The only official communiqué I've had lately was from Forest Enterprise talking about haulage contracts – I'm a sawyer, rather than a timber haulier, but they seem determined I run a wagon. If they'd thought to warn us earlier I might have been a bit more cautious when I sent fresh cut larch to a customer in Northumberland in the spring.

As a grower (and the Commission absolutely know I've got some larch growing locally) I'm equally in the dark. One planting is about a mile from a confirmed case, and I am watching it carefully, but I might just as easily be ignorant.

I have a nasty suspicion that if it ever was possible to confine the pox we've missed the boat. I hear it has already floated across the Bristol Channel, and is in South Wales.

HM GMO, and happy peasants

Whilst enjoying an early morning cuppa I was half listening to the silly old bird who twitters away (in the more conventional meaning of twitter that is), when she read out a report that Monsieur Sarkozy is only wanting short-arse security guards around him, to, er, lessen the contrast. Now yon radio bird observed that it seems to be OK to report on someone's height, when you wouldn't be permitted to define someone by their colour or, and I quote, 'sexism' – it's OK girl, we know what you mean. Such references were, she went on, actually height-ist. Fair point I thought (chuckling to myself about Terry Pratchett's 'equal heights' dwarf campaigners), before the nice lady went straight into a comparison between the heights of various World Cup footballers. Hmm, own goal there then Sarah? Bless her, she does like to stick her foot in it.

Mind, she is still less toe-curling by far than the old twerp who used to have the vaguely religious early slot on Sundays.

As you might recall, he became consummately proficient at interrupting the guests he was interviewing, telling them what they thought before they could answer. In the interests of equality he was 'encouraged' to bring members of other faiths into the studio, and he would often phrase questions that corrected their misguided and erroneous beliefs before they could even speak. It became, in latter years, almost worth listening to for just this dreadful treatment.

For the record, I don't suppose I could do better. Try phoning me at that hour on a Sunday, and see what sense you get! (No. On balance, I'll save you the bother. Phone me at that hour and all you'll get will be expletives.)

Anyway, back to the radio. We then got to the news, wherein a report advised of the planting of some genetically modified crop in (and again I quote) 'a high-security location'. Oh? And where could you plant GMOs for field trials in a high-security location? A vegetable patch in the grounds of the local prison perhaps? Maybe they've dug up the lawns at Sandringham? Perhaps her Majesty has struck a deal with some agri-science giant, utilising her secure grounds. There'll be less dependence on the civil list, and the experiment can be patrolled by an octogenarian armed guard – well known to have an itchy trigger finger – clutching a side-by-side Purdey, accompanied by a brace of rabid corgis.

Mind, won't it be awkward when security is breached by a pair of balaclava wearing eco-terrorists, intent on destroying the crop? One of this shadowy pair, known to the wider world only as 'Crusty Chas', might release the group's demands, reading from a written statement: 'One deplores the unsustainable behaviour of Mater…'

I'd better move right along from this line of thought, seeing, as many of you must know (and anyone could soon work out) that Alison and I rent Coaker Hall from a lovely ex-Navy chap who lives up in Gloucester, who is well known for his organic leanings (you know the fella, married that lass Camilla). Wouldn't do to upset 'em.

Sorry, before we do move along, I've taken a new tack with the never-ending stream of junk mail and unsolicited telemarketing calls. (We seldom get doorknockers any more for some reason. Shame really, I've got to buy food for the dogs now.) But anyone who phones trying to flog me double glazing, or sends a letter addressed to 'the home owner', is simply referred to the actual owner of the property. Curiously, few of them seem to think they'll have much luck, although one or two brighter ones quickly ask if I've got a phone number (which I haven't). I wonder how many enquiries get through?

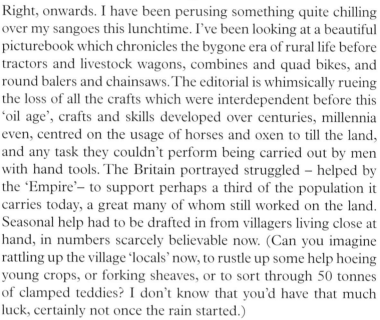

Right, onwards. I have been perusing something quite chilling over my sangoes this lunchtime. I've been looking at a beautiful picturebook which chronicles the bygone era of rural life before tractors and livestock wagons, combines and quad bikes, and round balers and chainsaws. The editorial is whimsically rueing the loss of all the crafts which were interdependent before this 'oil age', crafts and skills developed over centuries, millennia even, centred on the usage of horses and oxen to till the land, and any task they couldn't perform being carried out by men with hand tools. The Britain portrayed struggled – helped by the 'Empire'– to support perhaps a third of the population it carries today, a great many of whom still worked on the land. Seasonal help had to be drafted in from villagers living close at hand, in numbers scarcely believable now. (Can you imagine rattling up the village 'locals' now, to rustle up some help hoeing young crops, or forking sheaves, or to sort through 50 tonnes of clamped teddies? I don't know that you'd have that much luck, certainly not once the rain started.)

It's a beautiful book, looking at the countryside just a century ago, and realising how much of it is still visible, unspoiled, today is a warming thought. But whereas the pages of grainy old pictures of rows and rows of stooks and sheaves and ricks and faggots might look picturesque, as a peasant farmer I also saw the weeks and months of hard graft involved. I saw the hardened yellow hands of the folk who worked the land, and the shine on the handles of their tools.

It was starkly clear how far oil and technology has taken us from what actually was, more or less, sustainable. Do we have the vision to build a society, beyond fossil fuels, where we shall be able to live as we now like to live? That, my flower, is the big question.

As an afterthought, I did notice that despite being caught at their hard physical graft, and obviously having, and living on, very little, most of the subjects in the book seem happy enough with their lot. I wonder if their descendants, wherever they are, look as happy in their work today?

The author baling hay

How the wheels are greased

After a big flap around midsummer, when early cuts of grass on lower ground were found to be very short of volume, there's been a good deal of dampness on the higher ground. This has filled out the bottom of our remaining 100 acres of mowing ground into a very respectable sward. We've made a start on that now, and I suspect there's a good cut due if we can only get three dry days on the trot.

Whether this will alleviate the national forage shortage is another matter, but at least it'll mean I'm not quite so at the mercy of the wider trade. I'm anticipating trying to find about 30 tonnes of hay and 10 of feeding straw. My merchants are not, at the time of writing, phoning daily asking me to take the first load.

I did look carefully at wholecrop silage backalong, but the logistics of it didn't work. The nearest arable crops are about 10 miles away, and were being highly valued by midsummer. (I'd have thought selling a standing crop early, with no worries about subsequent weather/harvest, would be an attraction, but apparently the straw is being valued by the individual stem and measured in Troy ounces.) I'd have to travel a lot further than I could see the maths stacking up.

I gave up, and waited for some rain. If we really have a shortfall, and I can't find hay, then I'm simply going to lose some cows. I'm sure it'll all fall into place d'rectly.

I won't admit to putting by some reserves by way of sending the kids up some trees that needed pollarding, and pulling the nettles around the yard, chucking the resultant foliage in a loft. You wouldn't believe me, would you? Oh! You would believe me.

Onwards then. The pillock on the radio was very excited this week cos he was due to interview Brian Johnson, lead growler with Aussie rock band AC/DC. To indicate how excited he was, and to whet our appetites, he played a few chords from a couple of AC/DC tracks every 10 minutes. Not only is this an annoying habit generally, but I do wonder if someone ought to let him know that the songs in question – 'Whole lot of Rosie' and 'Highway to hell' – were recorded some years prior to Mr Johnson's arrival on the scene, before singer Bon Scott joined that celestial rock band in the sky.

When the interview finally arrived the DJ actually played one of the songs right through by way of introduction. Happily, the roguishly urbane Geordie, Johnson, brushed it off with hardly a mention. Perhaps he's used to it.

Moving smartly along, I was waxing lyrical the other day about the comparison twixt the new government's attitude to British Aerospace and that of the previous administration. You'll recall that recently cuddly Dave and his crew all decamped to India to help flog a few jet fighters for BAe. Compare that with the Labour lot, who were shocked and outraged backalong to uncover that some overseas (arms) deals might be secured with big cash bungs to various overseas ministers and officials. Shock, horror! (Personally, I never saw the problem.)

Giving it some thought later, I was trying to identify in which countries such bungs grease the wheels. For it is indeed the case that such behaviour, ranging from arbitrary 'on the spot' speeding fines, all the way up to – allegedly – wheels being greased for international arms deals, is absolutely the norm across much of the world.

Pretty much anyone who has travelled outside the tourist-resort enclaves of any African, Far Eastern, South American, or even Eastern European country will attest to this. Russia is notorious for it, and it's simply the way the world works.

You want examples? OK. A pal of mine is lately back from a few years working in an (un-named) Southeastern European country, which would very much like to join the EU please. He was project managing a flash property development, and assures me that local authority pretty much runs on cash bribes. Nothing could be even found in the Town/County Hall without a few dollars to help sniff it out, let alone stamped or approved. Sums ranged from a bundle in the back pocket up to suitcases full for big stuff. No one expressed any surprise, and the concept worked as an informal taxation system.

It didn't work very well mind, as my pal observed. When an area was being 'developed' the money poured in, builders rolled up, officials took their cut, and things went forward. Unfortunately, as an area becomes 'hot', a gold-rush mentality sets in and plans are approved all over the tranquil beauty spot before anyone considers what all the development will do for the vista. It takes, apparently, four to five years to cycle from a lovely leafy bit of coast, with a few quaint old fishermen sitting around a harbour unchanged for centuries, to a hi-rise concrete hell that no one would wish to live or holiday in.

By then, of course, the local officials have all buggered off.

My pal also buggered off, as the Bulgarian mafia was wanting to have a pretty serious chat with him about something or other (presumably for blocking the view from their concrete abomination with his).

Anyway, the long and short of it is that pretending it doesn't happen overseas is a bit naïve, and once out of Western Europe and North America you ought to expect it. I wonder if cuddly Dave knows this.

Doing something erotic to attract her

There's been something I haven't been able to fathom of late. Local jobbing builder, handyman and Jack-the-lad 'Des' (name changed to protect the innocent, or at least the 'acquitted on a technicality') has become great buddies with a local couple of the Earth Mother/lentil broth/hessian sandals persuasion. Now I must say I'm very fond of all parties, and they're all people for whom I've a lot of time, but… I just can't put 'Des' in the same social set as these gentle folk.

They're into native tribal chanting, he's a seventies' pop fan. They might peruse New Age papers on stone circles, Des reads

The Sun. They'll tuck into something novel with mung beans and rice, Des is more a bacon bap man (with ketchup).

Anyway, not being one to judge – or at least having enough knotty problems of my own – I just accepted their friendship at face value. Then, in a rare moment of lucidity, the penny dropped last week.

Our hirsute friends are much involved in the organisation of various music/spiritual festivals. Des dutifully attends whenever he can, tin of lager in hand. Of course! I realised, Des has heard all about this 'ere free love, and is now hanging about on the off chance that some tousle-haired dangling young thing might oblige. (And the best of British to you Des, I say.)

I only reluctantly share these conclusions to you, realising that various parties may very well, in the fullness of time, recognise themselves and come round to poke me in the eye. (Mind this is nothing to what the good Mrs Des will do, when the same thought occurs.)

Onwards. With the news full of France's rather controversial deportation of Roma gypsy migrants (and I openly admit to having just about no knowledge of what description should be used to describe which group, or whether any of them are actually ethnically identifiable, or if their differences are merely cultural. And no, I don't want my drive tarmacked), a couple of things caught my attention.

Firstly, when the subject kicked off in late summer I was trundling on a motorway journey, with the wireless on. To be topical the radio DJ played the Fleetwood Mac song, 'Gypsy', filling my mind with wholesome images of Stevie Nicks and that other bird, all floaty cheesecloth and whimsical bohemia. Mmm, nice.

As I got few miles on up the road, however, someone phoned in to describe their experiences with the legions of Roma kids – allegedly – begging at Paris railway stations, and their behaviour to extort travellers' cash. Rather less wholesome images I'm afraid.

Secondly, a few weeks later, some EU bigwig attacked the French government for this policy, likening it to the Nazi regime of the Third Reich 70 to 80 years ago. This was a pretty far-fetched comparison I'd have thought, given that the Frogs are merely trying to return these people to their country of origin. If my recollection of history lessons is accurate, the Nazis went just a little further. Denying the Roma were actually 'people' in the first instance was just the beginning.

I'm not going to condone or condemn Johnny Onion's behaviour ('go not to the Elves for advice, for they will say both yes and no'), but do try to keep it all in perspective, boys and girls.

🦟

Anyway, back on the ranch the real excitement is the boy's new Jack Russell puppy. Farmhand Joe has a lovely kind-natured bitch, and when he bred a litter we put our name straight on the list. John had been demanding a dog of his own – amongst many other things, mostly highly unsuitable – and we decided that, at age 11, the time has come. He has promised to be good 'forever'. Hmm.

There was some concern about the young collie bitch, which can be phenomenally bad tempered, and has to spend daylight hours in the house. (By all means, sneak into the yard in the dark. You'll find out why.) Anyway, the moment the pup appeared the collie loved it, licking it all over, and full of maternal care. Now we have to tiptoe past the terrier, in case she gets stood on and the collie counterattacks.

🦟

And a gag to close… we hope it's a gag.

Farmer Jack was round visiting farmer Jeff, but couldn't find him. Eventually, he heard music coming from the machinery shed. And therein, to the traditional tune, was farmer Jeff, doing a striptease in front of his Zetor. As Jack watched, Jeff whirled his old jacket around his head, and flung it up into the rafters. His flat cap already adorned a headlight. He flicked his wellies off the end of his toes into a pile of straw, and teasingly hooked a thumb in his braces. Clearly the trousers were next. 'Stop,' shouts Jack, unable to walk away, but horrified where this was going. 'What on earth are you up to, you old twerp?' 'Oh hullo mate,' says Jeff, unabashed. 'It's like this see, the missus and I, well, uz haven't been having a lot of luck upstairs together of late, so I went an' had a chat with ole doc Jarvis last week. He sez I gotta go and do something erotic to a tractor. D'you think this'll do?'

Polecats and foxhounds

When one of my semi-rural (as opposed to sub-urban) colleagues (who better remain nameless) was just a lad, he was out driving with his Dad. Suddenly the brakes went on as across the lane came scampering a sodding great polecat! Now old Dad saw the value of such a thing, the family being of that bent. (I believe you need a bit of polecat blood in your ferret line sometimes, like a touch of Swale in your Scotch ewes, to keep 'em sharp.) It had presumably escaped, but would certainly do very nicely in a cage in their back yard.

'Quick son, grab it, and chuck it in the back of the car. If we keep the windows rolled up it won't escape, and us'll get it home.' Junior leapt out and had it by the scruff in a jiffy. (This technique, like grabbing a snake, or possibly a tiger's tail, works just fine if you can keep away from the bitey end.)

Luckily, the lad got 'er slung into the back seat, and off they went again. Things were fine for a mile or two until Dad suddenly braked, swerving off the road and narrowly avoiding catastrophe. 'What's the matter?' 'Bliddy thing's bit me ankle boy, get it off!' This done, somehow, they did indeed get it home and transferred to a cage.

Sadly, as weeks went on, the cage proved hardly up to the job and the old polecat was frequently found missing, and had to be furtively recovered from around the neighbourhood.

Why furtively? Well these episodes curiously coincided with outbreaks of chicken shredding in back gardens all along the row of cottages. My pal played dumb as the neighbours steadily ran short of fowls, but he did have some sport with that old polecat along the way.

We've been off to another show – that'll be four this year... skivers that we are. John was allowed to drag/be dragged by Alison Bunning's very fine Riggit yearling round the ring once more (heifer from a very good home you understand). He hasn't get very far with her yet, but does enjoy the job. The heifer in turn is an absolute star, allowing anyone and everyone to fuss over her.

This show was one of those very convivial rural affairs where the stewards, punters and exhibitors seem to be one large extended group of chums. I have said before that such things are very special, and should be recognised as a treasure within our community.

As the late comers were unloading stock I was gassing with a steward pal (hello Nick) when, right in front of us, a Mum pulled up in her people carrier, decanted a small child from a passenger door, and the little girl's pet sheep from the boot. (A somewhat moth-eaten Speckle Face, looking like I'd sheared it, on a bad day, complete with purple spray around it's stern.) 'Hell's teeth, look at that,' muttered Nick. 'Hope the Trading Standards bloke doesn't see it.' I tapped him on the arm, discreetly nodding my head toward a gazebo going up right beside us, and in plain view of the little girl and her sheep. Sure enough, it was the Trading Standards Roadshow. Happily, the mush was embroiled with getting his placards arrayed how he wanted, and missed the spectacle. He then spent a long time scrubbing his boots with disinfectant for some reason. To be fair, we decided, if he'd noticed, and accosted the little girl (who was obviously as proud of her ovine charge as anyone present) he might never have left the field alive.

John showing Dory

I hadn't appreciated that the attached hound show was such a big bash. Packs attended from far and wide, and hounds of every type loped about in the *mêlée*, along with red coats trying to get them back in some sort of order – green coats for the beagles. We'd wondered on down with fellow Beltie breeders Anne and Will, who were a bit concerned by the dress code for spectators. This seemed to include cords and smart waistcoats, if not best suits. There were even blokes wearing pink corduroy strides, which is a very suspicious habit if you were to ask me – not that anyone does. My own outfit wasn't quite in keeping, including greasy steel toecap boots, grubby check shirt, and improvised knotted hanky (the obligatory 'red with white spots') to keep the sun off the old solar panel. I suspect someone should've asked me to move along if they'd been on the case.

Our local MFH, Mike, was there spectating. ('Never do very well showing,' he admitted. 'I work a bit of fell hound into 'em, and they never look showy enough.' Bit like showing cattle off Dartmoor then mate.) This did mean I could catch some of the judging with Mike as my ringside guide, which was very satisfactory. I know nothing of such matters, but he was able to explain what was going on, and the rationale – or otherwise – of the judging, and some of the dodges the stewards have to look out for.

He very kindly didn't mention my cultural attire.

Back on the cattle lines, later in the day, as we lounged under Alison Bunning's gazebo, loafing with cudding cattle sat half asleep, a reader of one of the publications I write for walked up, recognising me, and asked Mrs Bunning if she was the long-suffering Alison. This led to a certain local confusion, with my own Alison also present. For while Mrs Bunning may very well have her own crosses to bear, being married to me isn't one of them. Happily, matters were resolved without anyone taking offence, and introductions properly effected. The reader did ask if they'd be reading about the show… and indeed they may!

Getting your hands over a 4H

This back end time of summer brings the breeding cycle of the sheep round full turn once more. As the last of the lambs are weaned, thoughts turn to next year's crop. Will anyone notice if we sneak up to Scotland to the ram sales? Obviously, there are ram sales locally, but where's the fun in that, when we could just slip up the M6. (I should make it very clear – the whisky has nothing to do with this perfectly sound business planning.)

The ewes, meanwhile, have a couple of months to put on condition ready to make whoopee with the tups again. Mind, given that they'll 'live on the smell of an oily rag' at this time of year, you don't want to keep them too well. If they're too fat by autumn, they conceive fewer lambs. Admittedly, this is rarely the problem with the ewes on the high moors. For them, watching they're not too thin is more important. This'll be no better as they'll conceive even fewer and then not have the reserves to get themselves through winter, let alone bring forth lambs and milk.

So 'improving condition' is the goal, aiming for condition score 2–3 (on the industry 1–5 scale, with 1 being way too plain, and 5 being the opposite, with sub-divisions 'L' for light and 'H' for heavy).

I did, for a time, use this scale with a fellow shepherd to discreetly discuss the relative merits of lady bar staff. Sadly, we then ran into one of a rural bent who knew all too well the terminology. She took a damp bar towel to the pair of us when we murmured, in admiration, that she must be, at the very least, a 4H. (I should also warn you that once they're carrying a bit of fleece, you really need to put your hand on a sheep's lower back to gauge her condition, possibly grabbing her by the tail will suffice as well. I advise against the method for assessing young ladies, bar staff or otherwise, unless you are very sure of your ground.)

Perhaps now, in the era of celebrity status being everybody's yardstick, we could use a more up-to-date method of assessing a ewe's body score.

Obviously, we'd better not use individual names, but I think we could allocate job descriptions to give some kind of indication – and to help you grasp the old 1–5 scale I suppose.

At one end of the range would be the 'supermodel stature', sometimes adopted by aspiring starlets of other disciplines (unappealing to pretty much everyone's eye except, for reasons that remain unclear, those in the fashion industry). She'll struggle to hold to the tup, and we can all see she won't have the wherewithal to rear a lamb anyway.

Next up is that spare build of the 'long-distance runner'. Fit, if a little lean to have reserves for hard times. In a good year, she'll perform well

Still on the athletic vein, you get to the 'Olympic swimmer' build – of ewes, remember – who will perform as well as anyone, but is well found to handle a few harsh weeks through next winter. She'll rear you a double and make you proud, no worries.

Getting into the higher grades, you meet the 'daytime telly presenter' build, where good living and relative inactivity have graced a ewe with ample reserves to see her through a severe winter. She'll likely only carry one lamb, and if the going is easy next winter, it'll then be far too big to come out unassisted.

Lastly, we come to the 'McWimpy-King-customer-of-the-month' ewe, whose human equivalent only attains celebrity status when the 'drastic band' surgery goes horribly wrong. She hasn't reared a lamb for two years, and her good points are limited to the colossal crop of wool she clips, and the fact that she'll survive a 1947-type winter intact, coming out of a three-month-old snowdrift back down to supermodel build.

Now I'm aware that I may have upset some of you with these unkind comparisons. Perhaps I can address this with some useful lore on tup selection issues. A ram that's too skinny will soon be exhausted, and be of little use after a few days' at work, whereas an overly fat tup is likely to have to spend too much time lying in the shade, panting. No, what you'll be wanting is a tup that lives happily out on the hill, lean, but full of virility...
Sorry Ed, is this a bit near the edge?

Autumn 2010

Writing books

I was intending to tell you heart-rending stories of daring-do, how we've managed, finally, to get a reasonable crop of silage baled and stacked, and that some straw has arrived, complete with an oxygen mask for when I open the bill. I could fill you with admiration for our having snatched some late cuts of grass, in sticky horrid conditions, to ensure the cattle are fed this winter, or how even bales of straw that got rained right through have been heroically opened up, spread out to dry, and then re-baled.

On reflection though, I expect you've had your own weather-related activities, so we'll agree that it's been a sod of a summer again, between there being no rain when we needed it in May, and nothing but rain when we needed a dry spell to harvest. I know others have had worse luck still, and we'll offer our sympathy. So we'll raise a dram to having got through it, and we'll move right along.

Just now the media is full of reports on the extremely tacky 'Blair memoirs'. Although various aspects are attracting great excitement – and so far none of the sordid little fake's tales surprises me much – the bigger picture is how this is the norm for politicians.

Any kind of public service or high office seems to be a ticket to reveal all in a book, and frankly, my dear, that fills me with distaste. The previous government seems to be queuing up at the trough, some of them apparently planning their book launches prior to losing power. In fact, I'm beginning to suspect they might be aiming at 'the book' before they ever get elected. Isn't it all so seedy? Why can't they stick to dodgy directorships like in the old days? What's that? They do that as well? I see.

And as for poor Gordie's stab at the public speaking circuit, with one price for him, another for his poor Missus to speak as well – although she's only worth a fifth of his fee I note. Do they do a dance routine? Does he know some good gags? Cos I'd sure want something more for 100 grand than to listen to him drone on about his prudence – or lack thereof. It makes your toes curl.

Two-faced money-grabbing sell-outs, the lot of 'em. Funnily enough, I rather suspect some of the more earnest old lefties of yore might have something to say, if you like that kind of thing.

Something else that catches my pointy-nosed attention is the striking coincidence that so many 'celebrities' are also, apparently, such competent authors. This phenomenon goes right down to premiership footballers and talent-show stars, who give every appearance of hardly knowing which way up to hold a book.

I am confused. My wifey, who has been out in the wide world rather more than me, gently explained that what happens is that the blessed memoirs are actually written by something called a ghost writer, rather than the ex-minister/centre forward/ glorified showgirl. Oh? Isn't that a bit fraudulent then? (I have spent a minute or two trying to think of a worthwhile gag relating to ghost writers, but can't seem to get one together. Let me know when you come up with something.)

If it's any consolation, you may rest assured that this book is actually written by me myself. Much as I'd like to have some gopher do all the writing for me, I can't see it happening somehow. In fact it irks me somewhat that some spotty berk, whose saving grace is that he can kick a ball well enough to earn 50 grand a week, is then paid even more to pretend he's written his autobiography (I've never been tempted to delve into such books. I have to assume they are, cover to cover, a list of things a gullible young pillock can blow 50 grand a week upon).

Whether someone of 20 can have such a tale as to be worth telling is a moot point in itself. Unless he survived trotting up a Normandy beach in 1945, or stood in front of the French cavalry at Agincourt, or some such momentous experience, what could he tell us? Certainly, at that age, I was pretty much exclusively interested in how much lager I could contain in one go (and count myself very lucky to have had that opportunity).

Conversely, I have since been fortunate enough to have known an old German chap – now long gone – who, as a youth, was on a warship we torpedoed. He was in a complement of over 700, and suddenly there were only three left alive. That, and subsequent experience in the defeated 'Fatherland', had a pretty profound effect on a lad, still evident all those years later. Similarly, an Aussie I knew once – equally long gone – grew up in the dusty, desperate depression of the thirties, and had his character moulded in the most severe circumstances.

Extreme events had forged both of those old boys' characters, and they sure had some tales from their youth (and great is the pity neither wrote a book).

So, to round up this spider scrawl of thought, we will conclude that the next footballer who tries to sell us his story is first going to have to be starved, beaten, shot at, and thrown into the Atlantic, before we agree to read his wretched book. In fact, shouldn't we require the same of His Toniness? I'll pull the lever.

Aquatic sheep and train journeys

Being an unstoppable romantic, I've whisked my wife off on a three-day trip away. See, the Belted Galloway Society AGM and bull sale beckoned, and standing about a windy Scottish cattle market is such a heart-warming way to spend quality time together, isn't it?

Last year we drove up, arriving later than we'd like after getting buried in M6 traffic. The AGM and meal is the night before, and we somehow contrived to have to change into our glad-rags in the dark, in a lay-by on the A75. (God's teeth, she's a lucky girl is my wife.)

The previous year we'd flown up with Biggles and Algy in a wind-up plane. Between the stormy weather and my wife's issues with flying in small planes... well, it wasn't the most relaxed trip either. (Coming back, 'Cheapskate airlines' lent our plane to another set of passengers... really, we were about to board when we were sent off to another gate to watch a load of Brummies get on our kite. We spent a relaxing four hours waiting for the next one.)

Right, this year, we decided we'd try the train. The image was one of our relaxed arrival, having snoozed and read all the way, passing the time of day with our fellow travellers. No doubt these would be intriguing fellows with a keen repartee, unusual stories, and large bags of mint humbugs to share.

Sadly, the reality is rather different. For a start, the clever booking service allows 10–15 minutes for connections between trains, which is feasible in small stations where you can see the other platforms. It is less simple when you're a travelling hick, and lost in the sprawling Birmingham New Street. Obviously, when Casey Jones rolls in 20 minutes late anyway, you're in shtuck. We missed connections both up and back, but hey-ho.

As well as the joys of travelling to an unrealistic timetable, you're blessed with the actual travellers found on the trains, as opposed to the imaginary ones. While we were lucky at odd times, sharing topical discussion – about the alleged justification of Wayne Rooney's wages – with a rather affable old codger across the alleyway, we discovered the mongrel behind was an ardent fan, travelling from the Westcountry to pay £65 to watch Mr Rooney and his chums kick the techno equivalent to a pig's bladder about.

Frankly, I have experienced more stimulating company.

My hat goes off, however, to a nice lady we clocked on the way south again. She was very smartly presented, and I'd pegged her for an educated professional of a fairly high calibre. She sat down a row along from us, opposite an elderly lady of foreign extraction, who was travelling with her middle-aged son. Earwigging their conversation (to pass the time) I overheard most of this old biddy's life history – originating from Malta I believe – as she jabbered on, and all about how her son was almost a pro darts player (and he did indeed look like he might be an 'almost pro darts player'). Now the smart lady sat and chatted along with this pair, making polite chitchat all the while, for all of two hours. This was about one-and-three-quarter hours after you or I would have feigned nodding off (I wouldn't have been faking).

And damn me if it didn't turn out that the smartly turned-out nice lady, during a brief moment when her new best friend stopped to draw breath, was a farmer's wife from Lancashire. (Some arable, a lot of horticulture, grown daughters, and bound for Wilts/Hants someplace.) An ambassador of the highest calibre, and I salute you Madam. I rather think you should be gainfully employed at a rather higher level. Perhaps you already are, and your skills are just reflex now.

I'm sorry you hadn't found a seat with Alison and I. Then you could've chatted, with similar rapt interest, about the life and times of a peasant hill farmer.

On reflection, I have to face up to the reality that Madam might well have clocked the pair of us, and deliberately chosen another row.

Another facet of rail travel was exposure to fashions of the moment. All the rage, amongst young female passengers just now, are woolly black tights/tight black leggings. A skirt may be worn, but only if it is no bigger than you or I might imagine a belt.

Now obviously I'm all in favour of this fad, in certain instances. Again, it helps to pass time, when sat in cold damp stations. However, there are a marked number of devotees who also reflect a deep and abiding love of McDonuts, cola and chips. This makes said attire most ill-advised, and I could only think '4H, possibly 5', to be technical.

🦋

Anyroad, once up there we managed to secure a very smart two-year-old Belt bull. Our stock bull 'Mochrum Lonestar' is nine years old, and has daughters coming through. (He's now for sale. He's long, deep, has presence with impeccable manners, and was bred by the late Miss Flora Stuart, which is a higher accolade than anything I could say.)

We also got to stand with our pal Tim Oliver as he set a new record, paying £7500 for a Belt bull. Keep us a bull calf, mate.

🦋

Home again home again, jiggedy jig, and it's time to fetch the Scotch ewes in off the common for dipping and tupping. This involves a deal of extreme shepherding, and has already found me venturing far into treacherous bogs and wading across swollen streams to recover strays. It's a pretty hardcore way to farm sheep, keeping horn-headed ewes on such ground. Without a quad, it's the dog and me that do the work.

And Gyp wouldn't swim across said swollen river, as dusk was falling tonight, to fetch the lamb stuck on the far bank. He looked at me, head on one side, saying without words that he's not that stupid, Dad.

Mind, he only gets a handful of biscuit for his troubles, I'm about to seep my aching knees from within, with a substantial dram.

Fireworks

Recently I have taken the kids to a couple of fireworks shows. First up was Widecombe, where local pyromaniac Mark set off another astonishing display.

He's a jobbing builder really, but does like to put on his pointy wizarding hat and make some flashes and bangs. The locals all help out, and raise a bit of money for good causes. There's a pig roast in a marquee, with some foaming ale into the bargain. A group of the musically inclined get on a stage and do their thing, and it's all very jolly.

Sadly, this year, it chucked it down, which kind of dampens yer enthusiasm. With only the maddest kids – well, mine – running about outside, most of us crammed into the tent, waiting for the off. All credit to sparky heels Mark though; things still went off pretty spectacularly when he finally lit the fuse, or hit the button. He really is getting good at the job.

We'd all gone back out, and I was stood watching with another local Dad, Alex. He's a serving military officer chap, and has been spending a good deal of time somewhere dusty and, er, 'hot' of late. Knowing this, I asked him if he could calculate the distance to where the rockets were going off bang. Presumably, I rationalised, if you count from flash to bang, knowing light travels a lot faster than sound... 'Well, no,' admitted Alex, 'what actually happens, when you see the flash, is that you stick your face in the dust real quick.' (Ah, of course. What travels slower than light, but a lot faster than sound? Apparently it's likely to be whatever comes out of an AK47.)

Anyway, that was a fun, if soggy night out. A week or two later, an equally enjoyable – if rather less organised – display came round. The invites extended to a handful of households, and involved Farmer X (retired), Farmer X Jnr, and a small group of pals. Someone who'd better remain nameless had obtained a pile of 'professional display only' whizz bangs, which no doubt seemed like a good idea at the time. After a bit of nosh, and a drink or two, they were let off in a singularly unprofessional manner. Jnr did the lighting of the blue touch paper, in no particular order, with his Zippo lighter. Rockets went off in various directions, none of which seem to be planned, and mortars, which firmly insisted they were sunk into the ground before firing... er... weren't. A couple of them tipped over halfway through, sending remaining charges scooting across the field to go pop in a greatly exciting manner. They got cheers (Farmer X's safety concession? The 'littlies' watched from safe inside the French windows, 'big kids' could take potluck). There were a couple of neddies in a field nearby, who seemed to be quite excited by the whole show. One of the last rockets went off at 45 degrees, and exploded over their field, allowing them to share fully in the experience.

I was rambling away somewhere the other day how my post-FMD herd of Belts, White Galloways and Riggits is coming together very nicely now (I was in fact bemoaning the lack of profitable income from my cattle, but you hardly need to hear that). Now the interesting bit is the realisation that the cattle have come together much better than the hill ewes. Certainly, the sheep are also getting there, but nothing like as well as the cows. It's almost a decade now, isn't it? (Some drippy journo asked me recently if I'd realised that the 10th anniversary was coming up? She thought I mightn't have realised. Jeez Louise, it filled my waking mind for the longest time, and it was several years before the sound of the bolt guns finally left my dreams.)

The new Galloway herd was bought in piecemeal from pals. Not pedigreed, for the main part, but from people I know and trust. (Mostly, they're named after the ladies of the households they came from.) Putting my choice of bulls on them has started to give me a core of very respectable cattle once more, with a seriously smart bunch of heifers coming on stream now.

But the Scotch ewes, which were equally decimated, and the Cheviots, of which I lost the cream, I have struggled to get right. This autumn they are better than they've been, but they're still not there. Replacements were mostly bred up from the Cheviots I did have left, put to a wild-eyed Blackie ram born to one of the 36 original escapees. This meant, however, that I was keeping just about every ewe lamb, which is not a policy I'd advocate, and it's shown. I did bring in 30 Blackie ewe lambs from Tracey, and I purchased the odd strays that seeped in while we were emptied. They were all pretty good sheep, and have helped. I've been happy enough with most of the rams I've used since, but it's still taken a lot longer to come good than I'd wish.

It's a strange thing, and I bet I'm not alone in my experience. A hefted matriarchy of ewes, fit to live on a windswept hillside, isn't something you can buy off the shelf, and certainly doesn't come quick or easy, bred up from scratch.

I overheard an agent speculate, that fateful spring, that the valuation he'd just put on a nearby farmer's stock might seem like a lot, but would be the cheapest the farmer had ever 'sold'. Truer words I never heard.

Winter 2010/2011

Silver foxes

I'm not going to talk about the weather… I've already had way too much of it, and I've no doubt that you have as well. Suffice to say that if one more jolly twerp bounces up to me and says how pretty it all is, he faces a very real risk to his personal well-being. (Happily, few twerps actually get to bounce up to me as they haven't been able to negotiate the lanes for some weeks up here.)

I read with great pleasure that so many SFPs were made with such alacrity. Jolly good show chaps. Sadly though, and hardly surprisingly, ours seems, once more, to have slipped off the edge of the table, or possibly into a wormhole in the space–time continuum. I speculate (privately, so don't repeat it) that more 'substantial' payments are pulled out for 'further investigation' more often than smaller ones. What do you think? If you've got 5000 hectares of arable, in one unchanged block, I bet they're more likely to find problems to 'investigate', than if your claim were on your sole 4-hectare paddock (with numerous anomalies). The latter will go through unchecked, helping the declared statistics.

Is that the way it happens? (To be fair, it certainly would be if I were chancellor.)

Realising we were missed out once more, Alison phoned and got a lucid and very pleasant operative, no doubt hired especially to head off tetchy 'Alisons'. This operative tracked down someone who could promise that we had a dedicated case worker, and that he/she would phone us straight away… they'd just popped out of the office for a moment. 'Great. Thanks,' responded my beloved. Guess what happened next? That's right… not a squeak, and now we've got more immediate problems to attend.

Postscript A letter finally turned up, when a neighbour eventually got in to town to find the postie. The missive was telling us they didn't like the cut of our jib, so we were just going to have to wait, and we might as well stop blubbing about it. Interestingly, the letter was spectacularly bloodstained, although I understand that this was because the postie had slipped and cut himself, bleeding all over the van, rather than anything going on in the SFP dept.

And lastly, to broaden my mind, I've been reading about silver foxes. It might interest you to know that a Russian scientist in the 1950s took a bunch of these creatures from a fur farm, picking for their apparent docility, and subsequently bred them selectively for further increased docility. After a couple of decades he'd bred fawning tail-wagging 'doggies'. Their coat had changed, their ears flopped over, and they started breeding out of season – which they wouldn't ordinarily. They were essentially domestic dogs. The random sample, maintained during the same period, remained as cage-climbing snarling beasts. (Do bear in mind, won't you, that virtually every bit of domestic dog DNA comes from a very narrow line of wolf origin.)

The same scientist did similar experiments with rats, otters, and all sorts. One line of rats he separately bred for aggression, as well as the tameness selection, but going in the opposite direction. After a few generations one line was so tame you could take them out of the cage and stroke their sleek little backs – although, again, with coat changes becoming apparent. The other had become so vicious that chain-mail gloves had to be used to open the cage. One observer reckoned, should 10 to 20 get free, he'd fear for his life.

Sadly, much of this project's work was lost after the money ran out, following the break up of the Soviet Union. (One rather hopes the rats weren't just turned out!)

Mind, I'm conducting similar experiments with my Blackie ewes, trying to use only tups which can clear a five-bar gate!

The buyzz and the cheque

Some years ago – quite a few as it happens – I was a long-haired teenage tear-arse, and rode a motorbike. One day, rounding a bend on the road out over a local common, much too fast I suppose, I struck a Scotch ewe. Now this ewe came off very much the worse, and by her paint mark belonged to Farmer Brown.

With no small amount of trepidation (fearfully in truth, for he had a pretty fiery reputation) I rode straight on down to his farm to admit my sin. The household consisted of the widower patriarch, and his two middle-aged bachelor sons. Their sprawling farming operation took in several hundred Scotch ewes, a couple hundred black Galloways, and a fair herd of South Devons, spread far and wide from 1700 feet up over the

Forest of Dartmoor to the lush depths of the Dart valley and down into the South Hams.

On arrival, after I'd edged past the rabid collie chained to the table leg and confessed my sin, old Farmer Brown fixed me with his beady eye, and set a price on the sheep. No fuss, no dressing down. I wrote him a cheque there and then, and went on my way. (And this was, you'll understand, when the price of a young Scotch ewe was about the same as a farm lad's earnings for a fortnight.)

I came away smarting over the price, but grateful for the straightforward way the matter was dealt with.

Now fast-forward about 10 years. Farmer Brown and I are stood together at the ringside, at a dispersal sale. (The auction being precipitated by 'Jonathon Donuts' running out of beer vouchers, since you ask.) I had steadied up a fair bit in between, and was able to stand and chat at ease with such a senior farmer. He might've been a very old man by now, but I'd learnt just enough to hear what he had to say.

In fact, as I recall, the first thing he did was warn me I was about to lose some grass keep. He'd noticed an agent offering a farm on a local estate, with the benefit of an 'additional area of grass nearby'. The nosey old so-and-so had checked the acreage to work out where the grass was, and sure enough, my seasonal grazing agreement was on its way out.

Anyway, we chatted about this and that, and then he asked, in a famously deep brogue, 'Yere boy, 'ave you still got that modorbike?' 'Why, yes I have,' I replied. 'D'you remember you 'it one of my yaws one day?' he asked. 'Yes I do,' I responded, wondering where this line of questioning was going. 'And you come right down and give me a cheque,' Farmer Brown mused. My mind was racing: was the old so-and-so going say there was still something owing?

He went on, 'Lot of beggars' wudden've done that boy' he paused. 'You know I still get that cheque out and look at it sometimes.' I'd never noticed, but he couldn't bring himself to bank the cheque, seeing it was freely given.

This was a bit ironic, seeing as it was widely understood that those who evaded such settlements were tracked down and 'persuaded' to pay! Indeed it was suggested that if a cow was struck and left beside the road, Farmer Brown and the pair of sons toured local car-body repair shops until they found a Galloway-sized dent, then went to have a 'chat' with the owner!

Meanwhile, I had learned a couple or three good lessons from Farmer Brown, which have never left me.

❦

Now we'll pick the story up another decade on down the line. Farmer Brown has gone on, leaving his two sons (one of whom subsequently did marry, but was already in his sixties) to inherit the sprawling livestock empire. He'd also left £500 behind the bar of his local to ensure he was sent on appropriately, and I happen to know that the 'buyzz' had to top this up a fair bit to boot!

In amidst the paperwork the sons inherited, along with the Galloways, South Devons, and the Scotch ewes, was the cheque from 'young Coaker'. It lived behind the clock on the mantelpiece. I know this because whenever I had cause to visit the brothers , and raise a dram (for instance, when performing the annual 'returning of strays' rite) the cheque would be referred to – usually pulled out and examined even!

Despite, or possibly because of, their idiosyncratic ways, I became very fond of the brothers as years went on. They've made several guest appearances in my writings, in various anonymous guises, being such a rich fund of stories.

Something I've never described was Henry's reaction when we were first met after the 2001 incident (I'd lost my whole Galloway herd). He'd been away, and when we met on the road, in the narrows somewhere, he reached across through his open Land Rover window, with both hands, and gently took my hand. He spluttered and stammered, but couldn't find any words. Didn't need to. Just held my hand.

They carried on farming, although goodness knows how their agent kept them and their paperwork in order. They didn't exactly fit in DEFRA's plan. Jeez, they hardly fitted any mould, and the modern world just had to bend around them. Everyone who knew them will have their own recollections.

I've moved into the past tense, and am waxing lyrical now, because, as you've rightly guessed, the 'buyzz' have now both gone as well. They went in quick succession, without any lingering, and the world is surely a poorer place for their passing.

There being 'no issue' the business was steadily wound up. Many of the 'black cattle' are still to be found in amongst local herds, several still on the same piece of hill. Someone sorting out the paperwork has seen his or her way to returning my cheque, still uncashed. It sits on my mantelpiece now.

We're going to frame it and, just occasionally, will recall the Browns with a dram.

The author *Agnes Coaker*